PASSIONATE PRAYER

CATHERINE MARTIN

HARVEST HOUSE PUBLISHERS

EUGENE, OREGON

PASSIONATE PRAYER
Copyright © 2009 by Catherine Martin
Published by Harvest House Publishers
Eugene, Oregon 97402
www.harvesthousepublishers.com

Library of Congress Cataloging-in-Publication Data
   Martin, Catherine.
   Passionate prayer / Catherine Martin.
      p. cm.
   Includes bibliographical references.
   ISBN 978-0-7369-2378-1 (pbk.)
   1. Prayer—Christianity. 2. Devotional calendars. I. Title.
   BV215.M36 2009
   248.3'2—dc22

                                                      2008020675

Printed in the United States of America

          09 10 11 12 13 14 15 16 / VP-SK / 10 9 8 7 6 5 4 3 2 1

To Jim Smoke,
author, pastor, and my dear friend,
who has taught me about ministry and prayer,
and who has shown me by his very life and words
what it means to love the Lord
with all my heart, soul, mind, and strength.

ACKNOWLEDGMENTS

No book is ever written without the help of many. God gives the idea, guidance and strength in the writing. And then He brings a whole team of friends and family alongside to bring that book to fruition. I am so very thankful to Harvest House Publishers for their love for the Lord and excellence in every area, and especially to Bob Hawkins Jr. for his leadership and Terry Glaspey for his vision for my books. Bob Hawkins, Sr., I will be eternally grateful for the mark you have left on my life. A special thank you to Gene Skinner, my editor—you are simply the best!

My family has been so faithful to love and encourage me and pray fervently for me while I write. Thank you to David, Mother, Dad, Eloise, Rob, Tania, Kayla, and Christopher—I love you with all my heart. A special thanks to my dear husband, David, for your brilliant ideas and tireless help and encouragement.

Thank you to the wonderful staff team of Quiet Time Ministries—Kayla (my assistant at Quiet Time Ministries), Conni, Shirley, Paula, Cindy, Charlie—you are all such faithful servants of the Lord. Thank you to my friends who have taught me so much about prayer and have prayed for me—Beverly Trupp, Vonette Bright, Dottie McDowell, Andy Graybill, Leann McGee, Helen Peck, Kelly Abeyratne, Julie Airis, Stefanie Kelly, Myra Murphy, John and Betty Mann, Kathleen Otremba, and Sandy Rogers.

Thank you to the staff and women of Southwest Community Church. It is a joy to travel this road in life with all of you. Thank you to Shelley Smith, my assistant at church, for your service to the Lord.

Thank you to the board of directors of Quiet Time Ministries: David Martin, Conni Hudson, Shirley Peters, and Jane Lyons, as well as all of those who partner together with me in Quiet Time Ministries.

Thank you to Greg Johnson, my agent at WordServe Literary. I am so thankful for your wisdom and encouragement on this journey of writing.

And a deep thanks to Jim Smoke, my co-laborer in the gospel, for teaching me about prayer and being my great example of prayer.

CONTENTS

Week Four: Promises for Your Life of Prayer

Week Five: Passion for Your Life of Prayer

FOREWORD

As a child, I said my prayers in the morning at school, before meals, and on Sundays at church. As I think back, the Holy Spirit was stirring my heart and drawing me nearer to Him during those quiet times. In my twenties, I still prayed on Sundays at church, but my prayer life during the week had been reduced to "arrow prayers" here and there: *God, please help me with this...please help me with that.*

Then at age 29, when I broke my neck and became a quadriplegic, God truly became the sustainer of my life. My prayer with Him became a constant conversation. Sometimes I began the day praying, *Lord, I trust You with this new broken life,* and ended the day saying, *Thank You, Jesus, for getting me through this day.* On other days, I cried out, *God, I absolutely HATE living this way! I'm so mad!*

Yes, I did my share of arguing with Him. I wasn't suffering silently—that's for sure. At times, I questioned whether I should argue with the King of kings. But I likened my arguing with God to that of an immature, angry adolescent. Wouldn't parents rather listen to their teenagers scream and yell—as painful as that might be—than watch them run away from home for months at a time and go who knows where? My conversations with my heavenly Father may not have been the nicest, but they remained open and honest. I didn't run away. Eventually, I calmed down and began looking to the Lord for comfort, guidance, and joy. He certainly did not let me down.

Now, as a wife and mom, talking with God includes prayers like these: *Lord, my husband and I are tired. Will You place joy back into our lives?* Or *Lord, what high school should our son attend?* My prayer is often a time of praise and thanksgiving, acknowledging the greatness of our Creator. Some conversations are more intimate than others, but all remind me of the power that lies in talking with Christ, the great Comforter and Healer.

I first met Catherine Martin when she was kind enough to invite me to be the speaker for a women's event at her church in Palm Desert, California.

It was a beautiful spring morning. We immediately hit it off and found ourselves laughing and praying our way through the day. Something very powerful happens when you pray with a sister in Christ. I could sense the passion of her heart as she prayed that the women attending would open their hearts to Christ.

In *Passionate Prayer*, you will enjoy a wellspring of prayer experience from a woman who has walked with God for many years. She wisely states, "Prayer is God's prescription for a troubled heart. The more you pray, the more you experience God's peace." I have found this to be true in my life, and I'm sure you will find it to be true in yours. May the pages you read today jump-start your prayer life and turn it into consistent, honest conversation with the Prince of Peace, Jesus Christ.

Renée Bondi
recording artist, speaker, author

INTRODUCTION

When I graduated from college, I received a stylish set of luggage as a gift from my father. The memory of him giving it to me is so vivid that it seems as if it happened yesterday. I stood stunned and speechless in the university parking lot, still adorned in cap and gown long after the ceremony, as my father began pulling one piece of luggage after another out of his car and gave them to me. My heart raced. I was overwhelmed, not only by the gift itself, but also by what this gift meant to me in my relationship with God. That event became for me more than the celebration of achieving a bachelor's degree and more than a time of sighing relief and a few tears. Much more. My life of prayer graduated to a new and deeper level.

How could luggage take me to a new place in my prayer life? Well, lest you think me a girl easily impressed, please allow me to explain.

I had known the Lord for about two years. And for those two years, I had studied and investigated this great mystery of prayer. To me, prayer simply meant making requests of God. I saw prayer as me asking, Him giving, and me receiving. Prayer was in one compartment of my life. Studying the Bible was in another compartment. And worship was in yet another. Of the three, quiet times with the Lord became the greatest joy to me, and I could not seem to get enough time alone with God. I thought about Him all the time.

As I was nearing the end of my college years, I was invited to join the staff of Campus Crusade for Christ. You can imagine just how excited I was for this next step in my adventure with God. While I was driving home from Bible study one day, I allowed my thoughts to drift to my new life as a staff member with Crusade. I imagined what it might be like. The fun, the fellowship, the travel...travel? *Catherine,* I said to myself, *you don't have any luggage!* My heart sank, but I spoke a quick prayer out loud: *Lord, I'm going to need some luggage.* That was it. A thought. A simple prayer. And from that moment, I spoke with no one about my prayer borne out of my simple need.

I had grown up at home with my mother and my brother. Now, years later, my father and I are the best of friends, but growing up we didn't spend that much time together. So for him to come to my graduation and present me with a lavish gift was very impressive to me.

When I received the gift of an entire set of luggage from my earthly father and my heavenly Father, I was quite simply blown away by the person and presence of God—and the power of prayer. I realized in an instant that this need for luggage had been expressed in my mind in the presence of God Himself—I had been thinking with Him, walking with Him, and fellowshipping with Him. I had been merely thinking about life and my needs, sharing my thoughts with God. But more importantly, I knew God was listening. And subconsciously I knew He would respond. And this had been only about luggage—what about something really important? So you see why I was more than simply impressed by the luggage. I was stunned into a new awareness of what prayer can be.

Prayer was more than I thought it was—so much more. Prayer was more than listing out all my requests and looking for God to answer. Don't get me wrong; we are granted the incredible privilege of asking our Father for everything on our hearts. But think about it. In the best of any earthly relationship you have ever experienced, did you spend all your time together asking for things from that person? Of course not. Asking is only a small part of an intimate relationship. Prayer is so much more than we might know it to be on a superficial level. Prayer is *an intimate, ongoing, vibrant relationship with God that is nurtured through specific times alone with Him.* In short, prayer is walking and talking with God.

As the early church father Clement of Alexandria, said, "Prayer is keeping company with God."[1] Prayer is something we do all the time, in every circumstance, about everything. Ole Hallesby has said, "To pray is to tell Jesus what we lack."[2] That's why Paul challenged, "Don't worry about anything; instead, pray about everything" (Philippians 4:6 NLT), and "Pray all the time" (1 Thessalonians 5:17 MSG). When I caught this glimpse of the depth and delight of prayer, I was taken to a new and deeper level in my relationship with God. And more than that, I was motivated to spend more time with Him on a daily basis. My quiet time became rich, full, and satisfying as I was taken beyond the perspective of perfunctory ritual, rote exercise, or religious activity. I stepped into an intimate relationship with God Himself.

And dear friend, God desires the joy of a blessed relationship with you. At its deepest level, that is the purpose of prayer. It is a life devoted to a relationship with God. He writes His desire in broad strokes all across His Word. That's why He says, "Be still, and know that I am God" (Psalm 46:10 NIV). That's why Jesus said to His disciples, "Come away with me by yourselves to a quiet place" (Mark 6:31 WILLIAMS). In *Passionate Prayer,* we are going to take a journey into the delights of your intimate relationship with God. But even more, we are going to share together in the richness of growing deeper into this life of prayer. This deepening life of prayer is meant to be a passion for you and me, the lifeblood of our spirituality, forming the very fiber of our soul. The power of a praying life is unparalleled, for God is at work in such a life. The praying life depends on God and relies on His strength.

Why is the term *passionate* in the title of this book? Why not simply, *Prayer?* Passionate prayer is prayer from the heart. Passionate prayer takes you on an exciting adventure of conversation and communion from your heart to the heart of God. My goal for you is that your prayer life displays the powerful and compelling emotions of infinite love for God and boundless enthusiasm for prayer as a discipline. I see a life of passionate prayer as singing sweet music to the ears of the Lord. I see passionate prayer deepening your relationship with God through a prayer growth plan that can be individualized just for you. I see passionate prayer modeled from the wisdom of heroes of the faith and Jesus Himself. I see passionate prayer prevailing through the promises of God. I see passionate prayer empowering revival, intercession, and spiritual warfare.

Bill Bright used to tell this story:

> A man traveled to a certain city one cold morning. As he arrived at his hotel, he noticed that the clerks, the guests— everyone—was barefoot. In the coffee shop, he noticed a fellow at a nearby table and asked, "Why aren't you wearing shoes? Don't you know about shoes?"
>
> "Of course I know about shoes," the patron replied.
>
> "Then why don't you wear them?" The visitor asked.
>
> "Ah, that is the question," the patron returned. "Why don't I wear shoes?"
>
> After breakfast, the visitor walked out of the hotel and into the snow. Again, every person he saw was barefoot. Curious, he asked a passerby, "Why doesn't anyone here wear shoes? Don't you know that they protect the feet from cold?"
>
> The passerby said, "We know about shoes. See that building? It's a shoe factory. We are so proud of the plant that we gather there every week to hear the man in charge tell us how wonderful shoes are."
>
> "Then why don't you wear shoes?" the visitor persisted.
>
> "Ah, that is the question," the passerby replied. "Why don't we wear shoes?"

Bill Bright would then explain that when it comes to prayer, many Christians are like the people in that city. They know about prayer, they believe in its power, and they frequently hear sermons on the subject, but it is not a vital part of their lives.

There are many ways to experience depth in your life of prayer, but we will focus on a select few adventures. I am so excited to embark on this 30-day journey with you. I do not claim to be an expert on the subject of prayer. In fact, I am not certain anyone here on earth can make that claim. Certainly some men and women have engaged in the journey of prayer for many years. In fact, we will talk about some of the best books on prayer, written by those who have walked intimately with God. As I write this book, I sense a need to go deeper in my life of prayer. I hope you do as well. As Paul exhorts us and with God's help, may we set our minds on those things above, not on the things that are on the earth (Colossians 3:1-2). Let's venture into God's Word and see what God has to say to us about prayer.

HOW TO USE *PASSIONATE PRAYER*

Each week you will *read, respond,* and *experience*:

Read. In each day's reading, interact with the ideas by underlining what is significant to you and writing your comments in the margins. This book will help you walk and talk with God, relating with Him in every area of your life. Please mark it up and make it yours! You will also want to keep your Bible close by to look up those verses that mean the most to you on this 30-day journey.

Respond. To help you think through and apply all that is written here, I have included a devotional response section at the end of each day: You'll find a key verse to meditate on and memorize, questions for you to consider, and a place for you to express your thoughts and respond to what you have read. This is your opportunity to dialogue with God about your life of prayer.

Experience. A complete quiet time at the end of every week emphasizes the principles in that section. Use the blank Notes page to record what you learn from the companion DVD to *Passionate Prayer.*

Share your journey. Read what others are learning on their journey through *Passionate Prayer* and share your own insights with others throughout the world by posting your thoughts on the Quiet Time Ministries discussion board at www.quiettimecafe.com.

SUGGESTED APPROACHES

You can benefit from this book in several ways:

Sequentially. You may want to read the book a day at a time and implement the principles before moving to the next chapter.

Topically. You may have specific topics of interest to you. If that is the case, you can look at the table of contents and focus on those topics.

Devotionally. You may choose to read this book over 30 days. The days are divided into five sections so that you can take five weeks to read and think about prayer. It can be a 30-day adventure!

SUGGESTED SETTINGS

Personal and private. This is the kind of book you can read again and again. It will encourage you to draw near to God, especially if you have lost a habit of time with your Lord in His Word or you need to shake up your quiet time because it has become lackluster and routine. You might even want to spend some extended time with this book in a beautiful setting to revive and refresh your relationship with the Lord. It's a retreat in a book!

Small groups. I encourage you to travel on this 30-day journey with some friends. Sharing what you are learning with others who also love the Lord brings tremendous joy. Use the questions at the end of each day for your discussion together. More discussion questions are in appendix 1. This book may be used in Sunday school classes, Bible study groups, church congregations, or your family devotions.

Ministry spiritual-growth campaign. You may also desire to use this book as a 30-day intensive campaign to teach, revive, and inspire those in your ministry in the area of prayer. Using it as a campaign will help grow your ministry as new small groups are formed. For more information on using this book as a spiritual growth campaign for your group, visit these websites:

www.30dayjourney.com

www.passionateprayerbook.com

COMPANION RESOURCES

Quiet Time Notebook and Devotional Bible Study pages

Passionate Prayer Journal

Passionate Prayer DVD (includes six messages from me)

Passionate Prayer—A Quiet Time Experience (Harvest House, 2009) is an eight-week devotional Bible study in quiet-time format according to the P.R.A.Y.E.R. plan introduced in *Six Secrets to a Powerful Quiet Time* (Harvest House, 2005).

Now let's set out on this great adventure of prayer! And oh, what an adventure it is to walk and talk with God. No other life experience compares with intimate communion and conversation with the Triune God, the Creator of the universe. So, dear friend, grab your Bible, clear a space in your day, and take some time to delve into the great mystery and majesty of prayer. May God richly bless you.

PERSPECTIVE FOR YOUR LIFE OF PRAYER

Days 1–6

WHEN YOU HEAR HIS MUSIC

*Behold, I stand at the door and knock; if anyone
hears My voice and opens the door, I will come in
to him and will dine with him, and he with Me.*

REVELATION 3:20

od wants to share every area of your life, each and every day of
your life. He longs to walk with you and talk with you. His invitation to a life of intimate fellowship resonates clearly in the words of Jesus,
who announces, "Look, I stand at the door and knock." Imagine this Jesus
as He is described in Revelation, adorned in flowing robe and golden sash,
with eyes like flames of fire, beckoning you with His voice of many waters.
"If you hear my voice and open the door, I will come in, and we will share
a meal together as friends" (NLT).

Do you hear His words and take them into your heart, mind, and
soul? They are as beautiful music inviting you to respond in the harmonious song of prayer. All of God's Word is a melody that plays as music
from the Lord. The question is, can you hear His music? And if so, how
will you respond? When music plays, we can move to the rhythm and sing

the melody. The Lord is inviting us to walk with Him, moving in perfect precision as He leads and guides us. In this way, we share in His life. We are walking with God. And then, as we hear His music play, we sing in our heart to the Lord. When we sing, we are asking Him to share in our lives. We are talking with God. This mutual and intimate sharing of lives is best illustrated in the chapter's opening verse, where Jesus invites us to dine in intimacy with Him.

I like to think of prayer very simply as *walking and talking with God.* Prayer is the song of our lives lived with the Lord Himself as He plays His melody into our lives. And how does His music play? In and through His Word. I love to think of God's Word as music. And thinking about the Bible this way is scriptural. The Greek word translated "voice" in Revelation 3:20 is *phone* and means a sound or tone. And the Hebrew word translated "song" in Psalm 96:1 is *siyrah* and alludes to the lyricism of a choir. The psalmist said, "Your statutes are my songs in the house of my pilgrimage" (Psalm 119:54).

The Bible also speaks often about singing to the Lord. The psalmist said, "Sing to the Lord a new song; sing to the Lord, all the earth" (Psalm 96:1). Another psalmist said, "But each day the Lord pours his unfailing love upon me, and through each night I sing his songs, praying to God who gives me life" (Psalm 42:8 NLT). The sons of Korah said, "He's Lord over earth, so sing your best songs to God" (Psalm 47:7 MSG). Paul encouraged us to sing and make melody in our hearts to the Lord (Ephesians 5:19).

I grew up in a musical home, so I can relate to the musical metaphor to help me understand my own prayer response to God and His Word. I love to sing. And my favorite place to sing is in my car. My husband tells me I probably wouldn't sing in the car if I saw how funny I looked. I like to turn the worship music up really loud, so loud that in my own mind I sound just like the gospel artist.

One day while driving home from work, I was stopped on the busy interstate in rush-hour traffic. My Sandy Patty CD was playing with the volume turned full up. One of my favorite songs began playing—"Come, Let Us Worship the King." I know every word of that song. Because I was stopped in traffic, I could really concentrate on the music. I began gesturing to the music as I sang. I was so into the song that I *was* Sandy Patty. I held every note just like she did, and at the end, when her voice soared into the stratosphere as only Sandy Patty can sing, I was right there with her! I held the last note until *forever* just like she does, with my arms outstretched.

Just as the song ended, some movement in the car in front of me caught my eye. I want you to know I received a standing ovation. The man in the car turned around, smiled, applauded, and began laughing. I started laughing also, realizing how ridiculous I must have looked to anyone watching. Here's the point—I did not know anyone was watching. I was singing with all my heart to the music. The man in the car in front of me could not hear the music, so he could not respond and sing. He was an observer. I was a participant.

The world is full of observers. Every now and then, some people step out of the crowd, hear the music of the Lord, and respond, becoming active participants with Him. They walk and talk with God, engaging in lives of prayer. They share in the Lord's life, and He shares in their lives. The music comes from the Lord, through His Word applied by the Holy Spirit, constantly asking you to open the door of your life to walk and talk with Him. And when you walk and talk with Him, you pray—passionately and from the heart. George MacDonald says, "Communion with God is the one need of the soul beyond all other need: prayer is the beginning of that communion, and some need is the motive of that prayer. So begins a communion, a talking with God, a coming-to-one with Him, which is the sole end of prayer."[1]

In the midst of one busy season in my life, I received an emergency phone call alerting me that my mother was being rushed to the hospital. I packed some bags, jumped in my car, and drove to Phoenix. Over the next few days my life was consumed with this family emergency. I became overwhelmed with the pressure of responsibilities. The thought came to me, *Cath, you have not even opened your Bible. You have not spent any time with God for several days.* I was shocked because I love my quiet time with the Lord.

So I grabbed my *One Year Bible,* my devotional reading, and my Quiet Time Notebook, and I sought out a quiet place in a restaurant to draw near to God. I'm so glad I did. Guess what verse was in my Bible reading that day? Revelation 3:20. Those words took on new meaning. It was as though Jesus was comforting me and did not intend for me to go it alone in this trial. He longed for us to take the journey together.

My first response was *I'm sorry, Lord. Yes, let's share this trial together. Thank You for Your friendship and Your love.* And then I read the words of David in Psalm 131:1-3: "LORD, my heart is not proud; my eyes are not haughty. I don't concern myself with matters too great or too awesome for me to grasp. Instead, I have calmed and quieted myself…O Israel, put your hope in the LORD—now and always" (NLT). When I read those words, God seemed to be saying, "O Catherine, put your hope in Me now and always." I underlined the words *now* and *always*. I said to the Lord, *Thank You for comforting me. My hope is in You. I don't understand Your ways, but I trust that You have a plan and that You are not worried.* In just a short time, I had listened to the Lord's music in His Word, walked and talked with Him in prayer, and enjoyed an intimate time of fellowship.

I love these words by C. Austin Miles because they are so descriptive of our life of prayer.

> I come to the garden alone
> While the dew is still on the roses
> And the voice I hear falling on my ear
> The Son of God discloses.
>
> He speaks, and the sound of His voice
> Is so sweet, the birds hush their singing,
> And the melody that He gave to me
> Within my heart is ringing.
>
> I'd stay in the garden with Him
> Though the night around me be falling,
> But He bids me go; through the voice of woe
> His voice to me is calling.
>
> And He walks with me, and He talks with me,
> And He tells me I am His own;
> And the joy we share as we tarry there,
> None other has ever known.

Dear friend, how are you living your life? Do you walk and talk with the Lord? Do you share in His life? Do you include Him in all that you do? Can you wholeheartedly sing the last four lines in the poem above? May those words be the cry and commitment of your heart today.

DATE:

KEY VERSE: "Look! I stand at the door and knock. If you hear my voice and open the door, I will come in, and we will share a meal together as friends" (Revelation 3:20 NLT).

FOR FURTHER THOUGHT: As you begin this 30-day journey, take some time now to talk with the Lord about where you are in your relationship with Him and what you hope to gain from your time with Him in *Passionate Prayer*. Write a prayer to Him in the form of a letter in the space provided and then watch what He does in your life over the next 30 days.

MY RESPONSE: A Letter to the Lord

Day Two

THE RHYTHM
OF THE MUSIC

*Are you tired? Worn out? Burned out on
religion? Come to me. Get away with me and
you'll recover your life. I'll show you how to
take a real rest. Walk with me and work with
me—watch how I do it. Learn the unforced
rhythms of grace. I won't lay anything heavy
or ill-fitting on you. Keep company with me
and you'll learn to live freely and lightly.*

MATTHEW 11:28-30 MSG

The rhythm of your life determines your ability to pray. Most people live at breakneck speed with no time for thought, let alone prayer. Jesus does not walk at the fast pace of the world. And neither will you if you walk and talk with Him. He invites you to a new rhythm of life, easy and unforced. Remember that He says, "Come to me. Get away with me and you'll recover your life. I'll show you how to take a real rest. Walk with me and work with me—watch how I do it. Learn the unforced rhythms of grace. I won't lay anything heavy or ill-fitting on you. Keep company with me and you'll learn to live freely and lightly." The Greek word translated "rest" is *anapauo* and alludes to complete recovery and refreshment. We are meant to move with the ebb and flow of the tide created by Jesus as we walk and talk with Him through prayer.

I was privileged to attend a Christian Booksellers Association convention in Anaheim many years ago, before my own books were even published. What a fascinating experience to watch authors signing their newly published works. I remember stopping at one exhibit to get a signed book from one of my favorite authors. I told her how much I loved her books and asked her when a new book would be coming out. When she looked me in the eye, I could see she was very tired. She said, "I'm not writing anything right now. I need to soak in the Word of God for a while." I took those words to heart, and I have never forgotten them. She recognized the need for a change in rhythm—a sensitivity to the pace of Jesus in her life.

My mother studied to be a concert pianist, and while raising my brother and me, she taught piano lessons in our home. She used a metronome to establish the proper tempo of musical pieces for her students. Consequently, I've always known that proper rhythm and pace are essential in music. But I really learned anew the importance of rhythm when my husband took me to a Drum Corps International competition one summer evening in Riverside, California. I had never been to one of these competitions, and I was afraid it might be boring. Wow, was I wrong! It was one of the most exciting events I've ever attended.

After we found our seat in a packed college football stadium, I immediately sensed an air of excitement from all the loyal fans surrounding us. From the moment the announcer shouted the name of the first competitor to the second the gun exploded as the ensemble crossed the finish line, I seemed to have held my breath, my heart pounding in my chest. Flags twirled high in the air, horns reached searing highs, and drums pounded pulsating rhythms that shook the stadium. I've never seen or heard anything like it. Then came the Santa Clara Vanguard and the Concord Blue Devils, both past DCI champions. The stadium rose for one standing ovation after another. And what made the best ensembles so great was their ability to execute everything in absolute precision, the sum of all parts working together in perfect rhythm.

Pauses and rests are critical to any music. If you sing without rhythm, the song won't make sense. Similarly, your life requires a slowing of pace for balance, symmetry, and harmony. The Lord's rhythm is singular, distinctive, and different from the world's frenetic pace. The world says, "Keep working. Pack in as much as you can in the hours you have." But the Lord says, "in returning and rest you shall be saved; In quietness and confidence shall be your strength" (Isaiah 30:15 NKJV). There's the pause. He says, "Come away with me by yourselves to a quiet place and rest a little while" (Mark 6:31 WILLIAMS). There's the rest. Your life rhythm will develop as you keep in step with your Lord. He invites you to walk with Him and work with Him, learning His unforced rhythm. His desire is expressed in Jeremiah 3:19, where He says, "You shall call Me, My Father, and not turn away from following Me." In Matthew 4:19, Jesus said, "Follow Me." Again and again, His words invite you to *follow Him.* Walk with Him. Keep in step with Him (Galatians 5:25).

How can you develop a sensitivity to the pace and rhythm of the Lord? By establishing a rule of life that encompasses both your current responsibilities and your heart's need for quiet and solitude. Recognize the importance of a pace that allows for stillness—a time, a place, and a plan. You will stop your frenetic pace, look over your schedule, and create space for *a quiet time* alone with God. Don Postema, author of *Space for God,* speaks of his own challenge in finding time for talking with God. He says, "I used to write in my daily calendar '7:00–7:30 A.M.—Prayer.' But many times I passed that up. It was one more thing to pass by that day. Now I write '7:00–7:30 A.M.—God.' Somehow that's a little harder to neglect."[1]

And then, finding *a quiet place* will help you hear God speak in His Word. As a result, day by day, you will spend concerted time in this quiet place, locked away from the world, with your Lord commanding your attention. Finally, *a quiet time plan,* what you do alone with God, is not a legalistic ritual of do's and don'ts, but a proactive strategy on your part to retreat from the maddening flow of the world into Jesus' unforced rhythm of grace.

Please remember, you must be vigilant about your sensitivity to the Lord's rhythm of pause and rest if you would engage in a life of walking and talking with your Lord. The Lord gives you permission to engage in such a radical strategy of godly rhythm in life when He says, "Be still, and know that I am God" (Psalm 46:10 NIV). This is one of my favorite verses in all of Scripture; I think about those words every day of my life. I constantly remember that He is inviting me to stillness. It's not wrong of me to stop during the day to draw near to Him; it's essential. A.W. Tozer gives us this counsel:

> The man who would know God must give time to Him. He must count no time wasted which is spent in the cultivation of His acquaintance. He must give himself to meditation and prayer hours on end. So did the saints of old, the glorious company of the apostles, the goodly fellowship of the prophets and the believing members of the holy Church in all generations. And so must we if we would follow in their train.[2]

Perhaps as you read these words, such a graceful life seems a pipe dream to you. You might be thinking, *I have so many responsibilities each day. There is no room for the slightest pause.* I invite you—implore you—to set aside some time to stop and think about your life.

I have often had to make drastic moves to change my own hectic schedule. I work full-time as a women's ministries director at a church, and I speak and write for Quiet Time Ministries. I am a wife, a sister, an aunt, and a daughter. Each role in life involves time, energy, love, and attention. When I try to live in my own strength, I fail miserably. I become a basket case.

Believe me, I have tried to do it all in my own strength more times than I care to admit. What do I mean by that? Because there is so much to do, I reason in my own mind that if I just launch out and do it all without slowing down and taking time with my Lord, I'll get everything in my life accomplished and check off every item on my to-do list. What happens is that I become tired and worn out, and I lose any sense of spiritual well-being. I am thankful for the Lord's initiative in my life, constantly inviting me to draw near to Him. Those words in Matthew 11:28-30 are some of my favorites from the Lord. I hear Him saying, *Catherine, are you tired?*

I answer yes.

Are you worn out? Burned out on religion?

"Yes," I respond.

And then He says those words that are music to my ears: *Catherine, "come to Me. Get away with me and you'll recover your life. I'll show you how to take a real rest. Walk with me and work with me—watch how I do it. Learn the unforced rhythms of grace. I won't lay anything heavy or ill-fitting on you. Keep company with me and you'll learn to live freely and lightly."* These words from Jesus are so incredibly personal, inviting me to a new rhythm—one of grace, freedom, and confidence.

Entering into this new rhythm of Jesus is the beginning of a deeper life of prayer. Clement of Alexandria defined prayer as "keeping company with God." Keeping company is only possible when you step out of the rhythm of busyness into the rhythm of Jesus, where you find quiet and rest. Eugene Peterson, pastor and author of The Message, describes his own practice:

> I want to do the original work of being in deepening conversation with the God who reveals himself to me and addresses me by name...I know it takes time to develop a life of prayer: set-aside, disciplined, deliberate time. It isn't accomplished on the run, nor by offering prayers from a pulpit or at a hospital bedside. I know I can't be busy and pray at the same time. I can be active and pray; I can work and pray; but I cannot be busy and pray. I cannot be inwardly rushed, distracted, or dispersed. In order to pray I have to be paying more attention to God than to my clamoring ego. Usually, for that to happen there must be a deliberate withdrawal from the noise of the day, a disciplined detachment from the insatiable self.[3]

The vital question is whether we will step into a rhythm of life that provides a time, a place, and a plan to walk and talk with God.

One weekend I spoke to hundreds of women on personal, spiritual revival at a church luncheon in Phoenix. As always, I spoke on establishing a time, a place, and plan for daily quiet time. I showed everyone my quiet time basket and all my quiet time resources. There was excitement in the room at the prospect of time alone with the Lord. Driving home, I suddenly realized that even I needed to step anew into the rhythm of Jesus in my own life. The first thing I did was to take everything out of my quiet time basket. I put nonnegotiables back in, such as my Bible and my *Quiet Time Notebook.* But then I decided to add new devotional reading, new books on prayer, and even a new Bible reading plan with the *One Year Bible* in the New Living Translation.

The next morning, with a thousand things on my to-do list, I set them all aside and spent uninterrupted time with the Lord. I read His Word slowly, meditating on what He was saying. I underlined favorite phrases and verses with my pencil. I wrote thoughts and insights in my notebook. I read from my new devotionals and books. I talked with the Lord about what was on my heart. And when I finished, I was refreshed and ready to face the day. I experienced a real rest—rest for my soul. Stepping into the Lord's rhythm set my heart at the correct pace, one that was prepared and ready to face whatever came my way. I learned afresh what Paul meant when he said, "I can do all things through Christ who strengthens me" (Philippians 4:13 NKJV). And indeed, when you walk and talk with the Lord, you also will experience His strength, His joy, and His peace.

The soul is like a bird,
shaken from its peaceful roost by the inclement
circumstances of life,
where windblown branches
and sudden gusts from darkening horizons
thrust it into weather that is wild and uncertain.
And sometimes, however hard we beat our wings,
We can't seem to overcome the elements galing against us.
We are thrashed about in the air,
Windsheered and weary,
Wondering if our cries for help are reaching God.
But then the tempest subsides,
For a while anyway,
And the updrafts of God's Spirit lift us to new heights,
Above the wind, above the rain, above the earth.
And, for a moment,
We soar.[4]

KEN GIRE

DATE:

KEY VERSE: "Are you tired? Worn out? Burned out on religion? Come to me. Get away with me and you'll recover your life. I'll show you how to take a real rest. Walk with me and work with me—watch how I do it. Learn the unforced rhythms of grace. I won't lay anything heavy or ill-fitting on you. Keep company with me and you'll learn to live freely and lightly" (Matthew 11:28-30 MSG).

FOR FURTHER THOUGHT: How would you describe the rhythm and pace of your life right now? How can you step more deeply into the rhythm of Jesus and add pause and rest into your life to walk and talk with Him?

MY RESPONSE:

THE COMPOSER OF THE MUSIC

*But the Helper, the Holy Spirit, whom
the Father will send in My name, He will
teach you all things, and bring to your
remembrance all that I said to you.*

JOHN 14:26

K nowing our Composer, God Himself, is essential in our journey to a life of passionate prayer. The music of the Lord flows from all three persons of the Triune God—God the Father, God the Son, and God the Holy Spirit. The three persons of the Godhead always work in perfect synchronicity in your life as you pray. Your rhythm and your song respond and move in precision, ebbing and flowing from the Father, the Son, and the Holy Spirit as God carries out His plan and purpose. Jesus said, "But the Helper, the Holy Spirit, whom the Father will send in My name, He will teach you all things, and bring to your remembrance all that I said to you" (John 14:26). The Father, the Son, and the Holy Spirit spoke the music of the Word—the Bible—and we are blessed to have the opportunity to listen.

How does each person of the Trinity participate in the music of the Word? We know from Paul that "all Scripture is God-breathed" (2 Timothy 3:16 NIV), demonstrating its divine origin in God the Father. Peter tells us of the Holy Spirit's active role in the Word when he says, "For prophecy never had its origin in the will of man, but men spoke from God as they were carried along by the Holy Spirit" (2 Peter 1:21 NIV). Finally, John refers to Jesus, the living Word, when he says, "In the beginning was the Word, and the Word was with God, and the Word was God. He was in the beginning with God...No one has seen God at any time; the only begotten God who is in the bosom of the Father, He has explained Him" (John 1:1-2,18). God has spoken, and His music rings loud and clear, calling for a response from you and me. Will you move to His rhythm? Will you sing the song of prayer in response to His music? Will you walk and talk with Him?

Your prayer does not depend on you, but on God Himself. He is the initiator of prayer in your life. You might think of God as your eternal prayer partner. This depth of His involvement is vital for your understanding if you would walk and talk intimately with Him. The disciples asked Jesus the wonderful and powerful request that should become our request as well: "Lord, teach us to pray" (Luke 11:1). Jesus responded by saying, "When you pray, say: 'Father...' " (Luke 11:2). When we talk with God, we may direct our conversation to our heavenly Father. Jesus told those who heard His sermon on the mount, "But when you pray, go into your room, close the door and pray to your Father, who is unseen" (Matthew 6:6 NIV). According to Jesus, you have a Father who knows what you need before you ask Him (Matthew 6:8).

Jesus is also actively involved in your prayers as intercessor. We see in Hebrews 7:25 that "He always lives to make intercession" for you. Not only does He intercede, but He has already prayed for you. John 17:20 records His prayer: "I do not ask on behalf of these alone, but for those also who believe in Me through their word." We see in Hebrews that Jesus is our great high priest who sympathizes with our weaknesses, and He has been tempted in all things as we are, yet without sin (Hebrews 4:15). We are invited then to "draw near with confidence to the throne of grace, so that we may receive mercy and find grace to help in time of need." And who is at that throne of grace? Jesus.

He invites you to pray in His name when He says, "Truly, truly, I say to you, if you ask the Father for anything in My name, He will give it to you" (John 16:23). These words paint a picture of going to the bank of heaven with Jesus' name on our checks. Praying in Jesus' name is not an afterthought to our prayers, merely adding a religious phrase. It is a real resting on the merit of Christ for all your prayers to God. Praying in the name of Jesus means you rely on Christ's payment for all your sins, you depend on His unconditional love, and you draw from His unlimited credit in heaven.

The Holy Spirit is our helper or facilitator in our prayers. Paul tells us in Romans 8:26-27 that "the Spirit also helps our weakness; for we do not know how to pray as we should, but the Spirit Himself intercedes for us with groanings too deep for words; and He who searches the hearts knows what the mind of the Spirit is, because He intercedes for the saints according to the will of God." Do you see the strength and power at work on your behalf from God the Father, the Son, and the Holy Spirit? What a comfort and joy this truth should bring to you as you launch out in a new way in your life of prayer.

Early in my life of prayer, I wondered to whom should I pray—the Father, Jesus, or the Holy Spirit. I believe the Bible demonstrates that we may speak to all three. Paul prayed to the Father when he said, "For this reason I bow my knees before the Father" (Ephesians 3:14). And Jesus prayed to the Father when He said, "Father, I thank You that You have heard Me" (John 11:41). So, what about praying to Jesus? Jesus Himself invites you to come to Him (Matthew 11:28), to abide in Him and to have His words abide in you, and then to "ask whatever you wish, and it will be done for you" (John 15:4-7). In Revelation 3:20 Jesus invites us to open the door to let Him in that we might share a meal together with Him. Finally, we see by example in the Bible that we may communicate with the Spirit of God. Peter had a specific conversation with the Holy Spirit in Acts 11, and concluded, "The Spirit told me to go" (Acts 11:12). Another example follows from a letter written after the Council in Jerusalem recorded in Acts 15:28: "For it seemed good to the Holy Spirit and to us…" And then we see in Romans 8:16 that "The Spirit Himself testifies with our spirit that we are children of God."

Whether you direct your prayers to the Father, the Son, or the Holy Spirit, you can trust that all three persons are present, hearing your prayers and responding to you. At no time is there any separation, ambiguity, or dissension, for they are triune—three in one. The truth of the Trinity is a fact taught in Scripture, but it is also a mystery so great that no mind can comprehend it. As R.C. Sproul has said, "Some have argued that the doctrine of the Trinity entails a logical contradiction. However while the doctrine of the Trinity is a mystery to us, it is not a mystery to God, and is not a contradiction."

Don't be afraid of God, but fear (revere) Him. Don't distance yourself, but draw near. Don't abandon Him; instead, abide in Him. Join in the commitment of the psalmist in Psalm 42:8: "The LORD will command His lovingkindness in the daytime; and His song will be with me in the night, a prayer to the God of my life." In the music of God's Word you will learn new truths about who God is, what God does, and what He says. Your song of prayer will take on new melodies with each new truth you learn about Him.

This is one of my favorite prayers: *Father thank You for loving me and for sending Jesus as my Savior. Jesus, thank You for dying on the cross for my sins. And Holy Spirit, please fill me to overflowing with Your power to the glory of God.*

Three in One, One in Three, God of my salvation,
Heavenly Father, blessed Son, eternal Spirit,
I adore thee as one Being, one Essence,
One God in three distinct Persons,
For bringing sinners to thy knowledge and to thy kingdom.
O Father, thou hast loved me and sent Jesus to redeem me;
O Jesus, thou hast loved me and assumed my nature,
Shed thine own blood to wash away my sins,
Wrought righteousness to cover my unworthiness;
O Holy Spirit, thou hast loved me and entered my heart,
Implanted there eternal life,
Revealed to me the glories of Jesus
Three Persons and one God, I bless and praise thee,
For love so unmerited, so unspeakable, so wondrous,
so mighty to save the lost and raise them to glory.
O Father, I thank thee that in fullness of grace
Thou hast given me to Jesus,
To be his sheep, jewel, portion;

O Jesus, I thank thee that in fullness of grace
Thou hast accepted, espoused, bound me;
O Holy Spirit, I thank thee that in fullness of grace
Thou hast exhibited Jesus as my salvation,
Implanted faith within me,
Subdued my stubborn heart,
Made me one with him for ever.
O Father, thou art enthroned to hear my prayers,
O Jesus, thy hand is outstretched to take my petitions,
O Holy Spirit, thou art willing to help my infirmities,
To show me my need, to supply words, to pray within me,
To strengthen me that I faint not in supplication.
O Triune God, who commandeth the universe,
Thou hast commanded me to ask for those things
That concern thy kingdom and my soul.
Let me live and pray as one baptized into the threefold Name.[1]

My Response

DATE:

KEY VERSE: "But the Helper, the Holy Spirit, whom the Father will send in My name, He will teach you all things, and bring to your remembrance all that I said to you" (John 14:26).

FOR FURTHER THOUGHT: What is your most significant insight from your reading today? Take some time now and pray through the words of the prayer at the end of the chapter. Underline your favorite phrases from this prayer. Then close by writing a prayer to your Lord.

MY RESPONSE:

Day Four

YOUR SONG TO
THE LORD

*Be filled with the Spirit. Speak to one another
with psalms, hymns and spiritual songs. Sing
and make music in your heart to the Lord,
always giving thanks to God the Father for
everything, in the name of our Lord Jesus Christ.*

EPHESIANS 5:18-20 NIV

Prayer is your song to the Lord in response to His presence in your life. The psalmists knew the response of prayer as a song. Again and again they wrote words like these:

"I will sing to the LORD" (Psalm 13:6).

"He put a new song in my mouth" (Psalm 40:3).

"I will remember my song in the night, I will meditate with my heart, and my spirit ponders" (Psalm 77:6).

"Sing to the Lord a new song" (Psalm 96:1).

"The LORD is my strength and song" (Psalm 118:14).

"Your statutes are my songs" (Psalm 119:54).

"I will sing a new song to You, O God" (Psalm 144:9).

"Bless the Lord, O my soul! O Lord my God, You are very
    great; You are clothed with splendor and majesty...I will
    sing to the Lord as long as I live; I will sing praise to my
    God while I have my being" (Psalm 104:1,33).

You may speak the words of your song of prayer. You may hum the
thoughts in your heart and mind. Or you may literally sing your prayer out
loud to the Lord. However you walk and talk with the Lord, your prayer is
likened to a melody in your heart directed to your Lord. Paul said, "Be filled
with the Spirit. Speak to one another with psalms, hymns and spiritual
songs. Sing and make music in your heart to the Lord, always giving thanks
to God the Father for everything, in the name of our Lord Jesus Christ"
(Ephesians 5:18-20 NIV). J.B. Phillips translates this verse to read, "Let the
Spirit stimulate your souls. Express your joy in singing among yourselves
psalms and hymns and spiritual songs, making music in your hearts for
the ears of God!" I love that translation, for prayer is the voice that reaches
the audience of God Himself. God prompts your prayers, empowers your
prayers, and hears your prayers.

Why do we pray? There are five principle reasons: the *call* from God,
consecration to God, *communion* with God, *conversation* with God, and
cooperation with God.

First, prayer is our calling from God—it's how we obey God. He doesn't
just ask us to pray, He commands us! "Pray without ceasing" (1 Thessalonians
5:17). In fact, the Bible assumes prayer in our lives. God conversed with
Adam in the garden (Genesis 3:9-12). Jesus used the phrase "when you pray"
at least three times, assuming that we *will* pray (Matthew 6:5-7). The very
existence and being of God commands a response from us, thus making
prayer an imperative.

Second, prayer is our consecration to God—it's how we commit
ourselves to Him. Our devotion to God is seen in our prayers to Him.
Throughout the psalms you will notice this great resolve to pray:

"I will give thanks to the Lord with all my heart" (Psalm 9:1).

"In the morning I will order my prayer to You and eagerly watch" (Psalm 5:3).

"I will cry to God Most High, to God who accomplishes all things for me" (Psalm 57:2).

"Evening and morning and at noon I will pray, and cry aloud, and He shall hear my voice" (Psalm 55:17 NKJV).

Third, prayer is communion with God—it's how we walk with Him. God's desire for intimacy is not only written in His Word but also imprinted on our hearts through the indwelling Holy Spirit. Paul says, "For you have not received a spirit of slavery leading to fear again, but you have received a spirit of adoption as sons by which we cry out, 'Abba! Father!' The Spirit Himself testifies with our spirit that we are children of God" (Romans 8:15-16).

Fourth, prayer is our conversation with God—it's how we talk with Him. He talks with us in His Word, and we must respond if there is to be a two-way conversation. Our response to God is prayer. You discover this response and learn about prayer throughout Scripture itself. Many of the psalms are prayers and provide examples of how to pray. The psalmist said, "The LORD will command His lovingkindness in the daytime; and His song will be with me in the night, a prayer to the God of my life" (Psalm 42:8).

Finally, prayer is our cooperation with God—it's how we serve with God. When we pray, we join in ministry with the Lord. For reasons known only to God Himself, He has chosen to include us in His work by responding to our prayers and carrying out His plans and purposes. David expressed this amazing power of prayer to the Lord when he said, "I waited patiently for the LORD; and He inclined to me and heard my cry" (Psalm 40:1). Oswald Chambers says, "Prayer does not fit us for the greater works; prayer *is* the greater work."[1] Throughout the Bible, you will notice that when God's people prayed, God responded with supernatural, extraordinary power. (Read about Moses on Mt. Sinai in Exodus 33:18-23, Gideon and the Midianites in Judges 6–7, and Hezekiah and the Assyrians in 2 Kings 19.)

I believe God must be utterly shocked when we do not pray. How can I make such a bold statement? Three incidents in the Bible give me this impression about God's surprise at prayerlessness in the lives of His people.

When the people of God stepped away from Him and lived a life of immorality and oppression, God said, "I searched for a man among them who would build up the wall and stand in the gap before Me for the land, so that I would not destroy it; but I found no one" (Ezekiel 22:30).

I remember hearing a message on these words from Ezekiel many years ago and was profoundly moved to realize that God spent time looking for someone to pray for His people and found no one. I thought to myself, *Well, even if no one else is willing, I want to step up to the plate and pray for others so that the next time God is looking for someone, His eyes might rest on me.*

In Isaiah 65:1-2, God speaks about the rebellion of His people:

> I permitted Myself to be sought by those who did not ask for Me; I permitted Myself to be found by those who did not seek Me. I said, "Here am I, here am I," to a nation which did not call on My name. I have spread out My hands all day long to a rebellious people, who walk in the way which is not good, following their own thoughts.

In these verses, I see that God notices when I do not pray. I see the open and wounded heart of God, who is calling out to His people. These words embarrass me if I will not pray. To know that God is calling out to me for a relationship and yet to remain prayerless, to never talk with Him, is a sad estate that we must not allow in our lives.

Finally, I love the example of Samuel, who knew God and His view of prayer. On one occasion when the people were in danger from the Philistines, Samuel said, "Gather all Israel to Mizpah and I will pray to the Lord for you" (1 Samuel 7:5). The people begged Samuel, "Do not cease to cry to the Lord our God for us, that He may save us from the hand of the Philistines" (1 Samuel 7:8). God delivered the people in answer to Samuel's prayer. Then, when the people of God realized they had offended God by asking for a king, the people said to Samuel, "Pray for your servants to the Lord your God, so that we may not die, for we have added to all our sins this evil by asking for ourselves a king" (1 Samuel 12:19). Samuel's response reveals his understanding of prayer: "As for me, far be it from me that I should sin against the LORD by ceasing to pray for you; but I will instruct you in the good and right way" (1 Samuel 12:23). Samuel understood God's expectation of prayer in our lives. God wants this intimate sharing of our life and expects us to walk with Him and talk with Him about everything.

E.M. Bounds says, "Prayer moves the hand that moves the world." There can be no doubt that prayer makes a difference to God. You can know that when you pray, something powerful is going to happen. When Israel cried out to God in their suffering, God "looked upon their distress when He heard their cry; and He remembered His covenant for their sake, and relented according to the greatness of His lovingkindness. He also made them objects of compassion in the presence of all their captors" (Psalm 106:44-46). God relented concerning the calamity awaiting Ninevah when the people called earnestly upon God for forgiveness (Jonah 3:8-10). James clearly shows the significance of your prayers when he says, "You do not have because you do not ask" (James 4:2). According to James, "The effective prayer of a righteous man can accomplish much" (James 5:16).

In all these examples, we see the power of one prayer to our God. One prayer makes a difference with God and can ultimately impact people and nations. Always remember, God is looking for the one who will pray. May He find you and me offering that one prayer.

The Bible constantly teaches us about prayer and gives us numerous examples of prayer.

God is moved by our prayers (2 Samuel 24:25).

God listens to our prayers (1 Kings 8:28).

There are many postures for prayer, including kneeling and spreading our hands upward toward God (1 Kings 8:54).

God relieves distress in answer to prayer (Psalm 4:1).

We can pray out loud to the Lord (Psalm 5:3).

We should pray and then eagerly watch to see what God will do (Psalm 5:3).

We should pray when we are afflicted and needy (Psalm 86:1).

The psalmists often prayed in the morning (Psalm 5:3; 88:13).

God hears the prayers of the destitute (Psalm 102:17).

Prayer is like incense before the Lord (Psalm 141:2).

God delights in our prayers (Proverbs 15:8).

God hears our prayers and sees our tears (Isaiah 38:5).

We seek the Lord by prayer and supplications (Daniel 9:3).

Prayer is an act of devotion (Acts 6:4).

Prayer is a memorial to the Lord (Acts 10:4).

Fervent prayer accomplishes much (Acts 12:5).

We should pray for the salvation of others (Romans 10:1).

We are to be devoted to prayer (Romans 12:12).

We are to pray at all times in the Spirit (Ephesians 6:18).

Prayer should be given with an attitude of thanksgiving (Colossians 4:2).

Prayer includes entreaties, prayers, petitions, and thanksgiving for all men (1 Timothy 2:1).

We should pray night and day (1 Timothy 5:5).

Sometimes prayer is offered to God with loud crying and tears to God (Hebrews 5:7).

Prayer is to be offered in faith (James 5:15).

Your prayer can accomplish much (James 5:16).

We are to pray about everything (Philippians 4:6-7).

Constant prayer is the alternative to losing heart (Luke 18:1).

We are to pray according to God's will (1 John 5:14-15).

We are to pray without ceasing (1 Thessalonians 5:17).

Prayer in secret brings reward from your Father (Matthew 6:6).

We should often slip away to a quiet place and pray (Luke 5:16).

Prayer gives you spiritual strength (Luke 21:36).

The Spirit helps us pray in our weakness (Romans 8:26).

When you suffer, you should pray (James 5:13).

This list is not exhaustive, but these many principles about prayer taught in the Bible demonstrate how important prayer is to God and to us. Paul implores us to make the most of our time because the days are evil (Ephesians 5:16). One of the ways we use our time wisely is to pray.

In the early 1870s, not long after the disastrous Chicago fire, D.L. Moody traveled from Chicago to London while waiting for his church to be rebuilt. He spent his time listening to Spurgeon and other preachers. One day he attended a meeting in Exeter Hall on the Strand, and when visiting preachers were invited to share, Moody responded. After the meeting, a minister invited Moody to his church to preach the next morning and evening.

> I went to the morning service and found a large church full of people. And when the time came, I began to speak to them. But it seemed the hardest talking I ever did. There was no response in their faces. They seemed as though carved out of stone or ice. And I was having a hard time: and I wished I wasn't there; and wished I hadn't promised to speak again at night. But I had promised, and so I went.

That evening, Moody experienced the same lack of response in the beginning of his preaching. Then he describes an amazing occurrence:

> About half-way through my talk there came a change. It seemed as thought the windows of heaven had opened and a bit of breath blew down. The atmosphere of the building seemed to change. The people's faces changed. It impressed me so that when I finished speaking I gave the invitation for those who wanted to be Christians to rise. I thought there might be a few. And to my immense surprise the people got up in groups.

He preached for ten days to packed audiences, and more than four hundred people were added to that church. All the churches in the area were affected by Moody's preaching. Because of that experience, Moody realized his life work of preaching in areas beyond his own church, known as his "roving commission," marking the beginning of what we know as evangelistic crusades.[2]

Moody wondered about the explanation of the dramatic change in the church as he was preaching that first evening. He set out to discover the secret and was rewarded for his efforts. A woman who was a member of the church had become sick and was told by her physician that she would not recover but would be shut in her home for years. She lay there wondering what a life in bed for years would mean for her. She thought, *How little I've done for God: practically nothing: and now what can I do shut in here on my back?* And she thought, *I can pray.* And then, *I will pray.*

And so she prayed for her church. Her sister who lived with her gave her reports about the church. One Sunday at noon after church, her sister went into her room and said, "Who do you think preached today? A stranger from America, a man called Moody, I think was the name."

The sick woman's face turned white, her lip trembled, and she quietly said, "I know what that means. There's something coming to the old church. Don't bring me any dinner. I must spend this afternoon in prayer." And that night, God moved in a powerful way in the church.

When Moody visited this woman, she told him how two years before she had received a Chicago paper with one of Moody's sermons. When she read it, her heart burned, and she was led to pray that God would send Moody to their church. Just a simple prayer from a simple woman known by no one. She prayed for two years. And God brought Moody from Chicago to London to her church. All this was in answer to the prayer of a woman who dared to ask God for something only He could do. God loves a prayer like that. May we join her great company and dare to pray for extraordinary things and watch eagerly to see what God will do as we walk and talk with Him.

DATE:

KEY VERSE: "Be filled with the Spirit. Speak to one another with psalms, hymns, and spiritual songs. Sing and make music in your heart to the Lord, always giving thanks to God the Father for everything, in the name of our Lord Jesus Christ" (Ephesians 5:18-20 NIV).

FOR FURTHER THOUGHT: What is the most important truth you learned about prayer today? What was your favorite verse on prayer from your reading today? Will you join with the commitment of the psalmist and say, "He shall hear my voice" (Psalm 55:17 NKJV)?

MY RESPONSE:

Day Five

WHEN YOU
FINALLY SING

*Therefore repent and return, so that your sins may
be wiped away, in order that times of refreshing
may come from the presence of the Lord.*

ACTS 3:19

Prayer changes you. When you walk and talk with the Lord, you are transformed by His very presence. In Acts 3:19, Peter encourages his listeners to repent so that "times of refreshing may come from the presence of the Lord." Jesus says that when you come to Him, you will find "rest for your souls" (Matthew 11:29). The Greek word translated "refreshing" is *anapsuxis,* alluding to a cooling as with a refreshing rain in the summer heat. When you are refreshed and rested, your spiritual life grows. You are moved to pray for others. You find a new peace in a difficult situation. And you trust God for His work in your life. Eugene Peterson says, "We become what we are called to be by praying."[1] A.C. Dixon, the great preacher and pastor of Chicago's famous Moody Church in the early 1900s, declared, "When we rely upon organization, we get what organization can do; when we rely upon education, we get what education can do; when we rely upon

49

eloquence, we get what eloquence can do…but when we rely upon prayer, we get what God can do."

Oh, how our present generation needs to step away from the life of hurry and find the rhythm of walking and talking with Jesus. Most of the time when someone asks how we are doing, our response of "fine" really means, as one movie script put it, Freaked out, Insecure, Neurotic, and Emotional. But when we pray and move in the pace and rhythm of Jesus with pauses, periods, and rests, then our "fine" becomes Faithful, Inspired, Nourished, and Empowered. Faithful to God, inspired by Him, nourished by the Word, and empowered by the Holy Spirit. When we pray, the world can see the change in who we are and what we do.

And so, enriching our lives of prayer is worth the time and energy in order to move into that new rhythm that helps us to finally sing to the Lord. David, the man after God's own heart, discovered this truth when he was in the depth of despair. He was chased by Saul relentlessly for years, yet David possessed the promise to be the future king of Israel. Seeing no fruition of such a tremendous promise from God and forced to escape into enemy territory to flee Saul, David became discouraged. He cried out to God, "How long, O Lord? Will You forget me forever? How long will You hide Your face from me?" (Psalm 13:1).

Have you ever felt completely abandoned by the Lord? If so, then follow David's example. Cry out to God in prayer. That's exactly what David did. And David's prayer led him to trust in the lovingkindness of God. The transformation of David's demeanor is discovered in his subsequent words: "My heart shall rejoice in your salvation. I will sing to the Lord, because He has dealt bountifully with me" (Psalm 13:5-6). When you finally sing in prayer, you will be transformed.

Jean Giono, a French author, was mountain climbing in the French Alps in 1913 and was shocked to find barren mountains because of careless deforestation. Villages were abandoned because of dry brooks and springs. Giono happened upon a shepherd's hut, where he was invited to spend the night. He watched the shepherd sort through a pile of acorns, discarding any that were damaged or unusable. He learned that over the last three years, the shepherd had planted 100,000 trees with those acorns, resulting in 20,000 that actually sprouted. Years later, Giono visited the shepherd again and discovered the new growth of a vast forest as well as bubbling brooks, gardens, and flowers. He returned again after World War II and found the region glowing with health and prosperity. By sorting through piles of acorns and planting trees one day at a time, the shepherd brought new growth, forests, and fresh life.

When you pray, entire regions of your heart and soul and life are dramatically transformed through continuous times of refreshing. You may not notice a change in a day or a week. But wait and watch. You can *eagerly* look for such a renewal, as David says in Psalm 5:3: "In the morning I will order my prayer to You and eagerly watch." Then you'll see what times of refreshing and rest will do in your life. And you will see how the change influences the lives of those around you. Ole Hallesby, a Norwegian theologian, uses this image in his classic book on prayer:

> To pray is nothing more involved than to lie in the sunshine of His grace, to expose our distress of body and soul to those healing rays which can in a wonderful way counteract and render ineffective the bacteria of sin. To be a man or woman of prayer is to take this sun-cure, to give Jesus, with His wonder-working power, access to our distress night and day.[2]

Jesus says that when you walk with Him, you'll recover your life; that is, you'll find "rest for your souls" (Matthew 11:28-30). Do you need that kind of hope today? Then, dear friend, draw near and pray. Ray Stedman says, "Prayer is an awesome, mighty force in the world of men." May that force move in and through you to change the world.

O Lord, my heart is all a prayer,
But it is silent unto Thee.
I am too tired to look for words;
I rest upon Thy sympathy
To understand when I am dumb;
And well I know Thou hearest me.
I know Thou hearest me because
A quiet peace comes down to me,
And fills the places where before
Weak thought were wandering wearily;
And deep within me it is calm
Though waves are tossing outwardly.[3]

My Response

DATE:

KEY VERSE: "Therefore repent and return, so that your sins may be wiped away, in order that times of refreshing may come from the presence of the Lord" (Acts 3:19).

FOR FURTHER THOUGHT: The most life-changing prayer you will ever pray is the one in which you receive Christ into your life, establishing a relationship with God. If you have never asked Jesus to come into your life, then you may pray: *Lord Jesus, I need You. Thank You for dying on the cross for my sins. I ask You now to come into my life, forgive my sins, and make me the person You want me to be. I pray in Jesus' name. Amen.*

Or do you need a time of refreshing in your life? What have you learned today that encourages you to enrich your life of prayer and walk and talk with your Lord? Close your time today by writing a prayer to Him, expressing all that is on your heart.

MY RESPONSE:

Day Six

QUIET TIME
WEEK ONE:
THE PRIVILEGE
OF PRAYER

Devote yourselves to prayer.

COLOSSIANS 4:2

PREPARE YOUR HEART

One of the greatest privileges you've been given is the high privilege of prayer—walking and talking with God Himself. You've seen this week that the Bible has much to say about prayer. As you draw near to God in quiet time, you are going to look firsthand at some of those important verses and learn about prayer. Turn to God now and ask Him to quiet your heart and speak to you in His Word.

READ AND STUDY GOD'S WORD

1. In the Sermon on the Mount, Jesus taught His audience about God's perspective of prayer and what prayer really means. Read the following passages of Scripture and write what you learn about prayer:

Matthew 6:5-15

Matthew 7:7-12

2. Read the following verses on prayer and underline those words and phrases that mean the most to you:

"If you abide in Me, and My words abide in you, ask whatever you wish, and it will be done for you" (John 15:7).

"Be anxious for nothing, but in everything by prayer and supplication with thanksgiving let your requests be made known to God. And the peace of God, which surpasses all comprehension, will guard your hearts and your minds in Christ Jesus" (Philippians 4:6-7).

"Devote yourselves to prayer, keeping alert in it with an attitude of thanksgiving" (Colossians 4:2).

"First of all, then, I urge that entreaties and prayers, petitions and thanksgivings, be made on behalf of all men" (1 Timothy 2:1).

"Therefore, confess your sins to one another, and pray for one another so that you may be healed. The effective prayer of a righteous man can accomplish much" (James 5:16).

"For the eyes of the Lord are toward the righteous. And His ears attend to their prayer" (1 Peter 3:12).

ADORE GOD IN PRAYER

Talk with the Lord today about your desire to learn all about prayer and grow in your life of prayer.

YIELD YOURSELF TO GOD

Prayer is a daring venture into speech that juxtaposes our words with the sharply alive words that pierce and divide souls and spirit, joints and marrow, pitilessly exposing every thought and intention of the heart (Hebrews 4:12-13; Revelation 1:16). If we had kept our mouths shut we would not have involved ourselves in such a relentlessly fearsome exposure...Praying puts us at risk of getting involved in God's conditions... Praying most often doesn't get us what we want but what God wants, something quite at variance with what we conceive to be in our best interests.[1]

Eugene Peterson

Prayer is something deeper than words. It is present in the soul before it has been formulated in words. And it abides in the soul after the last words of prayer have passed over our lips. Prayer is an attitude of our hearts, an attitude of mind. Prayer is a definite attitude of our hearts toward God, an attitude which He in heaven immediately recognizes as prayer, as an appeal to His heart. Whether it takes the form of words or not, does not mean anything to God, only to ourselves.[2]

Ole Hallesby

Enjoy His Presence

How would you define prayer? What have you learned about prayer this week that will help you walk and talk with God more?

Rest in His Love

"Ask, and it will be given to you; seek, and you will find; knock, and it will be opened to you. For everyone who asks receives, and he who seeks finds, and to him who knocks it will be opened" (Matthew 7:7-8).

Notes—Week One

Week Two

A PLAN FOR YOUR
LIFE OF PRAYER

Days 7–12

Day Seven

YOUR PRAYER
GROWTH PLAN

_With all prayer and petition pray at all times in
the Spirit, and with this in view, be on the alert
with all perseverance and petition for all the saints._

EPHESIANS 6:18

Enriching your life of prayer requires purposeful planning and attention. Moving to a deeper level in the actual practice of prayer necessitates a dedicated time of devotion. While reading through Ephesians 6 in my quiet time, I came to verse 18, and the words _at all times_ seemed to flash in neon lights from the page. I firmly believe that when God wants to teach us something in the Word, the Holy Spirit opens our spiritual eyes, highlighting Scripture so we will see its truth for our lives. The eyes of my heart were enlightened (Ephesians 1:18) to see the importance of prayer in my life that day. I read Paul's words as though I had never read them before: "With all prayer and petition pray at all times in the Spirit, and with this in view, be on the alert with all perseverance and petition for all the saints." Do you know what word was most significant to me? A little word with big meaning—_all._ I knew from my pastor at the time that "all means all, and that's all, all means." In one broad brush stroke, the Holy Spirit used this verse to open up my mind and heart to see that I needed to grow deeper and more passionate in my life of prayer. I knew instantly that my life fell far short of such a life of *all* prayer, *all* petition, at *all* times, with *all* perseverance, and for *all* the saints. That little word *all* pointed to passionate prayer. I saw it as a "walking and talking with the Lord" that never stops, flowing from a heart of devotion to God. R.A. Torrey said that when the intelligent child of God stops to weigh the meaning of these words in Ephesians 6:18, he or she is driven to say, "I must pray, pray, pray. I must put all my energy and all my heart into prayer. Whatever else I do, I must pray."[1]

How could I step up to the plate, so to speak, and hit a home run in this new arena of prayer? How could I develop such passionate prayer with power? I made a radical, Holy Spirit–driven decision. I decided to design a prayer growth plan for myself with the guidance of God through His Holy Spirit. The Holy Spirit is the one who guides us in prayer and empowers us from within (Acts 1:8; Romans 8:26-27; Ephesians 5:18). In my case, the Holy Spirit led me to enroll in the school of prayer with serious intent and purpose.

Paul said, "Run in such a way that you may win" (1 Corinthians 9:24). Paul's words encouraged me to seriously consider the steps I take to grow spiritually in my relationship with the Lord. Paul encouraged his disciple Timothy, "Discipline yourself for the purpose of godliness" (1 Timothy 4:7). This level of Pauline discipline is the training necessary for unhindered pursuit of God's purposes. I'm a firm believer in training to be, as Oswald Chambers says, my utmost for His highest. That's one of the reasons why I sought a seminary education. And that's why I just knew, deep in my heart, after reading Ephesians 6:18, I needed a comprehensive prayer growth plan. I wanted to learn how to pray with the same fervor that Jesus' disciples had expressed in their request, "Teach us to pray" (Luke 11:1).

Where was I to begin in developing my prayer growth plan? In developing a life of prayer, I first asked myself these most basic of questions: When would I pray these passionate prayers, where would I pray as Paul described in Ephesians 6:18, and what would be my plan for growth in this life of prayer? I had already established a consistent quiet time by setting aside a time, a place, and a plan, so I already knew the answer to the first question. I realized my growth in prayer would occur best in the context of my quiet time.

To establish a daily quiet time, first set aside a time to be alone with the Lord. The time is best when you are alert and when you can have some uninterrupted moments with your Lord. Jesus often rose early in the morning to pray (Mark 1:35). I prefer the mornings, so that was settled. And then you need a quiet place for a time of communion with the Lord. Organize all your quiet time materials in your quiet place. I like to use a quiet time basket for my *Quiet Time Notebook,* my Bible, devotional reading, prayer helps, worship music, my hymnbook, pencils, pens, and reading glasses. You may have a bookshelf, a file drawer, or a briefcase. It's up to you. To draw near to the Lord each day, I use the P.R.A.Y.E.R. Quiet Time Plan:

Prepare Your Heart

Read and Study God's Word

Adore God in Prayer

Yield Yourself to God

Enjoy His Presence

Rest In His Love[2]

Then I needed to choose a tool to help me grow in this life of passionate prayer. Many years ago, I designed the *Quiet Time Notebook* to use in my quiet time. Then I revised the *Quiet Time Notebook* for others at the outset of Quiet Time Ministries. I have discovered that using a notebook with topical sections is a perfect reminder of all I can do in my quiet time. One of the sections in the *Quiet Time Notebook* is Adore God in Prayer. I had been using these Adore God in Prayer pages in my notebook to keep a record of my requests and God's answers to my prayers. (See the example in figure 1.)

First, I reviewed how I write out my requests: the date, a promise in Scripture (written from memory or chosen from a Bible concordance), and my actual request. I encourage you to put down in words your most important requests so you can keep a record of the amazing ways God answers your prayers. You can use a notebook like mine, a wire-bound notebook from any office-supply store, or a page in your journal. The point is to take

Adore God in Prayer

Don't worry about anything;
instead, pray about everything.
Philippians 4:6 NLT

Prayer for ___Bible Study___

Date: 6-20-08   Topic: Rev. Study
Scripture: Deuteronomy 31:8
Request: Father, prepare our hearts for our study this coming
         year. Transform our lives with Your Word this year.

Answer:

Date: 8-30-08   Topic: my teaching
Scripture: James 1:5
Request: Lord, please give me wisdom as I study and prepare
         our discussions. Give me a listening ear, sensitive to
         Your guidance.

Answer:

Date: 9-15-08   Topic: class
Scripture: Acts 17:11
Request: Lord, put it in the hearts of the students to study
         hard seeking You with all their hearts and souls.

Answer: 9-30-08 Thank You, Lord, for these great students

Date: 10-1-08   Topic: prophecy
Scripture: John 16:11
Request: Lord, give us understanding into the prophecy of
         Daniel, especially the 70 weeks.

Answer: 10-15-08 Thank You for showing us Daniel 9:25-27

Figure 1

time to record your most important requests. Writing will help you think and focus on the nature of your prayers, and you will see more clearly how God answers your prayers.

Second, I reviewed how I went about praying. Once you write your prayers take time to return to those prayers. This will help you with patience and persistence. You will probably forget many of your requests if you don't write them down. Always remember that God does not forget your prayers. He will answer, and He delights in your worship and thanksgiving in response to answered prayer.

Finally, I reviewed how I track God's answers. I like to record answers with a red or green pen to distinguish them from the requests. I am constantly amazed at the incredible ways God has answered almost every request I've written in my *Quiet Time Notebook*. In my Adore God in Prayer section, I sometimes organize my prayers topically. Here's an example:

Sunday—pray for your church.

Monday—pray for your country.

Tuesday—pray for the world.

Wednesday—pray for your community.

Thursday—pray for missionaries and other ministries.

Friday—pray for your ministry.

Saturday—pray for revival in the church.

And then I use a daily prayer page for my family and others. I use my Adore God in Prayer pages in a variety of ways. The pages have a flexible design with space for four separate requests. This enables you to focus on one person or situation, depending on your present need (see figure 1). I sometimes use a page to focus on one person in my life, praying daily for that person as the Lord leads. I can add new requests each day or each week. Or I can use a page to focus on a seemingly impossible situation burdening my heart. When I am in such a trial, I write out my requests day by day as I am in the Word of God. I will ask God for extraordinary answers to impossible situations. And the Lord helps me wait patiently for His answer.

So writing out my prayer requests on the Adore God in Prayer pages was the starting point for my new prayer growth plan. I thought, *Now I want to go deeper and focus on specific areas to grow in.* I prayed over a list of considerations: the importance of learning to talk with God, the use of Scripture, the various types of prayers in the Bible, learning from others, writing my own prayers, expressing and tracking my prayer growth, and knowing the character of God. Then I looked to the Bible as my university of prayer with four classrooms that will teach me how to pray: the psalms, the promises, the prayers, and the people. With these ideas in mind I developed the Passionate Prayer Growth Plan—eight new areas to help me grow in my life of prayer. And I designed eight journal-style prayer pages to add to the Adore God in Prayer section of my notebook:

Prayer Journal

Scripture Prayers

Listening to God

Thank You, Lord

Quotes on Prayer

Books on Prayer

My Adventure in Prayer

My Adventure in Knowing God

Over the course of this week, I want to share this prayer growth plan with you. You can use a journal or blank notebook pages to apply all that you learn. In fact, you may even want to take eight pages in your journal or notebook and title each page with one of the areas mentioned above. Then you will have a page in your notebook ready to use as the Lord leads you. Over the next few days, you will find examples of each aspect of your prayer growth plan to help you discover how you can apply it to your own life. I encourage you to have fun with these ideas as you learn and grow in prayer. This plan will encourage you to add pause and rest into the rhythm of your life, focus your attention on your intimate relationship with God, and as a result, pray about everything in your life.

Where should you begin? Remember, growing in your life of prayer is a lifelong adventure. And I want to encourage you to use this prayer growth plan as the Lord leads. You won't apply everything all at once. In fact, you may try these different ways to grow in prayer over the course of months or even years. I want to share them all with you now to give you some new and different ideas that have meant a lot to me over the years. I invite you to focus on one aspect of prayer, choose one idea from the prayer growth plan, and make that a part of your quiet time.

For example, if God shows me a great verse to pray back to Him, I'll focus on Scripture Prayers and write that verse as a prayer. If a particular verse becomes very important to me and seems to be highlighted by the Lord, I'll write it out, focusing on Listening to God. As my heart is filled with gratitude on a particular day, I will write out what I am thankful for, focusing on Thank You, Lord. If I come across a great quote on prayer, I'll write it out on the Quotes on Prayer journal page. Of course, I do not use all the aspects of my prayer growth plan every day. Start with one and grow with the others.

Ask yourself these questions periodically: Am I praying? Do I talk with God throughout the day? Do I have a regular quiet time when I can talk with Him about the burdens of my heart? Do I ever open the Bible? Do I have a time, a place, and a plan for my quiet time? What is that plan? Do I ask God before making major decisions? All of these questions will help you grow in prayer. In some seasons, you won't notice any growth at all. At other times, you will discover you have grown ten feet tall.

After many years of using this prayer growth plan, I can truthfully say that God has given me a deeper devotion to Him and a joy I simply can't keep to myself. Jesus said, "If anyone is thirsty, let him come to Me and drink. He who believes in Me, as the Scriptures said, 'From his innermost being will flow rivers of living water'" (John 7:37-38). The rivers of living water flow deep and powerfully in the lives of those who will dare to draw near to God in passionate prayer.

Lest we become overwhelmed that a life of prayer could be boring, tedious, and tiresome, let's remember the blessed companionship Jesus and His disciples knew. They enjoyed great moments of laughter, smiles, and sharing of meals. These were the norm. And they can be ours too when we walk and talk with the God who loves us.

Chuck Swindoll tells the following story:

On one occasion, evangelist Dwight L. Moody had been the recipient of numerous benefits from the Lord. In his abundance, he was suddenly seized with the realization that his heavenly Father was showering on him almost more than he could take. Encouraged and overwhelmed, he paused to pray. With great volume he simply stated, "Stop, God!" Now that's *spontaneous.* It is also a beautiful change from, "Eternal, almighty, gracious Father of all good things, Thy hand hath abundantly and gloriously supplied our deepest needs. How blessed and thankful we are to come to Thee and declare unto Thee…" and on and on and on, grinding into snore city. After I had told that story in one service, a fellow said to me, "I've got another one for God. God, start! I mean, He can stop on Moody, but I want Him to start with me, I need some of that."[3]

Will you pray together with me for the deepening of our lives of prayer over the course of these 30 days? *Lord, we lay ourselves before You and ask You to give us a new song for You, a heart for deep and passionate prayer and devotion. Will You, dear Lord, enrich our lives of prayer and bring great glory to Yourself? We ask this in Jesus' name. Amen.*

DATE:

KEY VERSE: "With all prayer and petition pray at all times in the Spirit, and with this in view, be on the alert with all perseverance and petition for all the saints" (Ephesians 6:18).

FOR FURTHER THOUGHT: Why is it important to have a prayer growth plan, and how will it help enrich your life of prayer? Why are you looking forward to growing in your life of prayer? Close by writing a prayer to the Lord, expressing what is on your heart today.

MY RESPONSE:

Day Eight

LEARNING TO
TALK WITH GOD

*Ask, and it will be given to you; seek, and you
will find; knock, and it will be opened to you.
For everyone who asks receives, and he who seeks
finds, and to him who knocks it will be opened.*

MATTHEW 7:7-8

God desires the act of prayer to be an animated, fervent, two-way discourse. He has already initiated the perpetual conversation with you through His Word, and now He awaits your resolute and constant response. You have been given an audience with the all-powerful, all-knowing Creator of the universe. What will you say? How will you talk with Him? Jesus says, "Ask, and it will be given to you; seek, and you will find; knock, and it will be opened to you." In this short sentence of instruction, Jesus encourages us with three emphatic imperatives: *ask, seek,* and *knock.* We are to be persistent in voicing our needs, persevering in sharing our thoughts, and unabashed in opening our hearts to our heavenly Father. In my journey, I set as my goal to learn how to speak with words that convey what is deep within my heart. As I formulated my prayer growth plan, I sought ways that would help me become more open and vulnerable with my Lord, the one who already knows what is in my heart (1 Samuel 16:7).

More than 20 years ago, I heard Josh McDowell give a powerful, insightful message that I've never forgotten. He urged those of us who were listening to bring everything on our hearts out into the light. In his message, Josh taught that when we pour out every single desire of our hearts to the Lord, we will experience a new depth in our life of prayer. As such, Josh boldly proposed that as we walk in the light of the Lord and bring our requests out into His light, we may be surprised at the results. Sometimes our circumstances don't change, but we do. And sometimes we see our desires broadened in scope and vision to encompass God's plans and purposes for a lost world. In my mind I can still see Josh sweeping his arm out in front of him, his voice rising, and saying, "Bring it out into the light!" Transparency with God can only deepen our intimate relationship with Him. The imagery of Josh's message showed me that my prayer growth plan needed to allow for openness and vulnerability in my conversation with God.

PRAYER JOURNAL: WRITE A LETTER TO THE LORD

The very first idea that came to my mind for my prayer growth plan was to simply write out my prayers. I use a page in my *Quiet Time Notebook* entitled Prayer Journal for the purpose of expressing all that is in my heart. (See figure 2 for an example.) You may use a page in your journal or notebook to write your prayers. I liken the act of writing prayers as writing letters to the Lord. In this way, I visualize Him reading all I have written. God will lead you as you pray. When you write your prayers, you might even view them as your own psalms to the Lord.

In fact, you may even write your prayers as poetry. You will be amazed at some of the prayers that you are led to write and pray. One I have prayed frequently has been instrumental throughout my life: *Lord, may my dreams and desires be hemmed in by the boundaries of Your plans and purposes.*

Writing out your prayers to the Lord has biblical precedence. The psalms are filled with written prayers, and David is one of the finest prayer writers in history.

Prayer Journal

Pray in the Spirit on all occasions
with all kinds of prayers and
requests.
Ephesians 6:18 NIV

Write your own prayers to God. Pray about everything on your heart,
including people, circumstances, trials, temptations, responses to God's
Word, and worship, praise, and adoration of God.

3-25-07 Lord, I pray that You will keep my heart soft and sensitive
to You and to others. May my eyes stayed fixed on You even when I
am distracted. Help me to run the race You've set before me with
endurance. May You be glorified in my life no matter what I face
today. As David says in Psalm 18, I love You, O Lord my strength!

4-6-07 Lord, I need strength today to keep the schedule that I
have. Help me, Lord, in every meeting to shine for You and love
others with Your love. Keep my words encouraging and help me to
point others always to You.

4-10-07 Thank You, Lord, for the incredible privilege to walk with
You in life. You have given me everything I need. Even in the midst
of my difficult circumstances, You are my strength and my refuge.
I always have a place to run, as Corrie called it, a hiding place.
Thank You, Lord, for giving me significance and purpose in life.

Enriching Your Life of Prayer © 1998, 2008 Catherine Martin

Figure 2

To You, O LORD, I lift up my soul.
O my God, in You I trust,
Do not let me be ashamed;
Do not let my enemies exult over me…
Make me know Your ways, O LORD;
Teach me Your paths.
Lead me in Your truth and teach me,
for You are the God of my salvation;
for You I wait all the day (Psalm 25:1-2,4-5).

Can't you just hear David's heartfelt passion for God reverberate from the pages of his written prayers? This is the reason I have dedicated this book's companion volume—*Passionate Prayer: A Quiet Time Experience*—solely to the rich wealth of prayer in the psalms.

What do you write on your Prayer Journal pages? Paul says, "First of all, then, I urge that entreaties and prayers, petitions and thanksgivings, be made on behalf of all men, for kings and for all in authority, so that we may lead a tranquil and quiet life in all godliness and dignity" (1 Timothy 2:1-2).

What do you write on your Prayer Journal pages? Paul says, "First of all, then, I urge that entreaties and prayers, petitions and thanksgivings, be made on behalf of all men, for kings, and for all authority, so that we may lead a tranquil and quiet life in all godliness and dignity" (1 Timothy 2:1-2). You may include entreaties (supplications)—urgent heartfelt requests based on a deep need, prayers—general requests in communion with God, petitions—intercessory requests on behalf of yourself or others, and thanksgiving—praises for blessings and benefits. You may also wish to make confessions—agreements with God about your sin (1 John 1:9). And you may write out commitments and resolves—decisions of attitudes or actions toward the Lord (Psalm 31:7).

SCRIPTURE PRAYERS: WRITE GOD'S WORD AS PRAYERS

The next essential for our prayer growth plan is personalizing verses from the Bible as our own prayers to the Lord. I use a Scripture Prayers page so that the Bible becomes one of my prayer partners. (See figure 3 for an example.) You may use a blank page in your journal or notebook to write out your Scripture prayers. This type of prayer has been called *lectio divina* or contemplative prayer. *Lectio divina* is Latin for "holy reading," intended to engender communion with the Triune God and to increase the knowledge of God's Word. Please understand that I am not advocating experiential mysticism. The crucial point here is that the object of your prayer is God and His Word, not self and the world.

John instructs us in 1 John 5:14-15 that we may be boldly confident in our prayers if we pray according to God's will: "This is the confidence which we have before Him, that, if we ask anything according to His will, He hears us. And if we know that He hears us in whatever we ask, we know that we have the requests which we have asked from Him." At a meeting of the Fellowship of Christian Athletes, Bobby Richardson, former New York Yankee second baseman, offered a prayer that is a classic in brevity and poignancy: *Dear God, Your will, nothing more, nothing less, nothing else. Amen.* We can know we are praying what is truly God's will when we pray using His Word itself. Dietrich Bonhoeffer points out that "if we wish to pray with confidence and gladness, then the words of Holy Scripture will have to be the solid basis of our prayer...The richness of the Word of God ought to determine our prayer, not the poverty of our heart."[1]

I find the psalms especially conducive to praying the Bible to the Lord. Here are two examples:

> *Lord, You are my shepherd. Because of You, I shall not want. You make me lie down in green pastures; You lead me beside quiet waters* (based on Psalm 23:1-2).

> *Lord, You are my light and my salvation; whom shall I fear? You are the defense of my life; whom shall I dread?...Lord, I want to ask You for one thing: and I seek it from You. I want to dwell in Your house all the days of my life, to behold Your beauty and to meditate in Your temple* (based on Psalm 27:1,4).

Some of my favorite prayers are paraphrases of Scripture:

Have mercy on me, a sinner (Luke 18:13).

Fill me with Your Spirit, Lord (Ephesians 5:18).

Who am I, O Lord? (1 Chronicles 29:14).

Revive me, O Lord (Psalm 119:25).

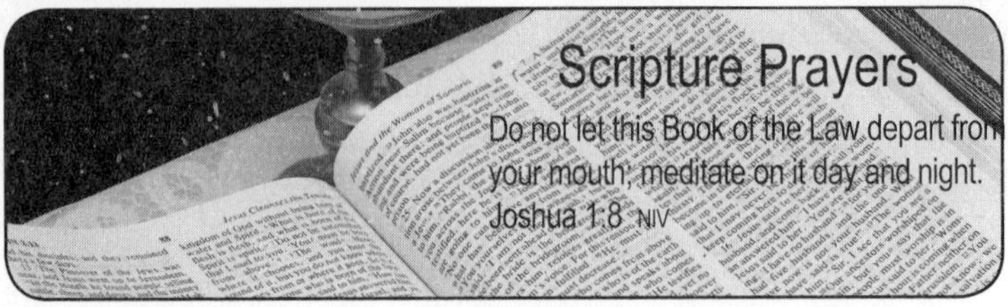

Scripture Prayers

Do not let this Book of the Law depart from your mouth; meditate on it day and night. Joshua 1:8 NIV

Write your own prayers, using verses and prayers in the Bible, applying the words to your own life circumstances.

Bible Verse(s): *1 Corinthians 15:58*

Lord, I pray that You will keep me steadfast, immovable, always abounding in Your work, knowing that my toil is not in vain when it is done in You.

Bible Verse(s): *Colossians 1:9-12*

Lord, I pray that You will fill me with the knowledge of Your will in all spiritual wisdom and understanding, so that I will walk in a manner worthy of You, to please You in all respects, bearing fruit in every good work and increasing in the knowledge of You; Strengthen me with all power, according to Your glorious might, for the attaining of all steadfastness and patience. I joyously give thanks to You, who has qualified any who know You (including me) to share in the inheritance of the saints in Light.

Enriching Your Life of Prayer © 1998, 2008 Catherine Martin

Figure 3

One marvelous tool that has helped me pray the Word of God is from the *Praying God's Will* series by Lee Roberts.[2] I encourage you to use a phrase, a verse, or even an entire passage from your Bible reading each day to prompt your prayers to the Lord.

LISTENING TO GOD:
WRITE WHAT GOD HIGHLIGHTS IN HIS WORD

Listening to what God says in His Word is another essential in your prayer growth plan.

I use a Listening to God page for my *Quiet Time Notebook* to emphasize the synergy between God's Word and thoughts, ideas, and actions that the Lord brings to my mind. (See figure 4 for an example.) You may use a page in your journal or notebook as you listen to God. The writer of Hebrews tells us that "the word of God is living and active and sharper than any two-edged sword, and piercing as far as the division of soul and spirit, of both joints and marrow, and able to judge the thoughts and intentions of the heart" (Hebrews 4:12). Listen for God's voice in His Word. Silence and solitude are important starting points in your approach. Mother Teresa has said, "God is the friend of silence—we need to listen to God because it's not what we say but what He says to us and through us that matters."[3] We listen for God not in a mindless vacuum, but in the context of His Word.

The Holy Spirit knows our struggles and where we are wrestling with God's ways in our lives. I remember a time when I felt so alone that I was tearful every moment of the day. I read Psalm 45:10-11 and paraphrased it in my notebook: "Listen, daughter; the King loves your beauty." This passage is a love song about the king and his bride, and is also thought to point to the love Christ has for the church. As I read those verses on a lonely day, I was reminded of the love Christ has for me and how He sees me as beautiful. I realized how close, intimate, and ever-present my Lord always is with me, regardless of how remote I may imagine myself. In those quiet moments, listening to God, I was greatly moved and encouraged by my Lord.

Sometimes my time with God will prompt an idea to encourage someone or an idea for ministry. I like to write those ideas on my Listening to God page and then pray for God to lead and guide me in their development. I'll never forget writing out what God taught me from the four

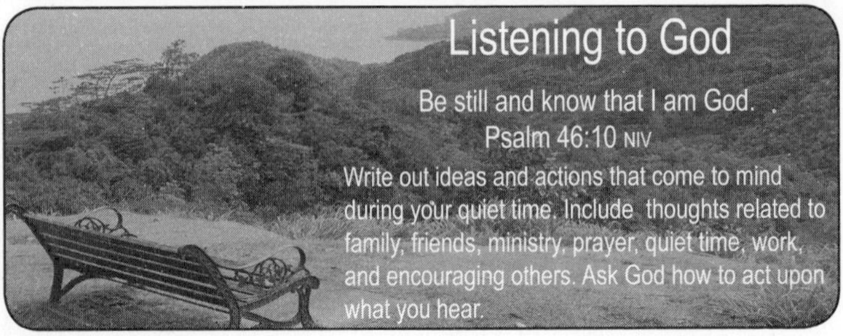

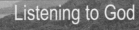

Listening to God

Be still and know that I am God.
Psalm 46:10 NIV

Write out ideas and actions that come to mind
during your quiet time. Include thoughts related to
family, friends, ministry, prayer, quiet time, work,
and encouraging others. Ask God how to act upon
what you hear.

Date: 3-25-08   Idea, Thought, or Action

This morning in my quiet time when I read Hebrews 4:12 about
how the Word of God is alive and powerful, I thought about how
we should always encourage others to be in the Word. Then I
thought about how to encourage my family with the Word of
God. I got the idea to get a new Bible for my niece—the kind
that will be easy for her to read. I'll make a quiet time basket for
her to get her excited about spending time with the Lord.

My Response: This is such a great idea! Why didn't I think of it
before! I'll take it to her when I visit next weekend.

Date: 3-28-08   Idea, Thought, or Action

Reading in Ruth 2:1-23 today was very powerful. I thought about
how Ruth was gleaning in the fields of Boaz, her kinsman
redeemer. I see this as such a picture for me of living and
gleaning in the fields of my Lord Jesus, who is my Redeemer. I
love verse 8 where Boaz says, "Stay right here with us...don't go
to any other fields." The Lord calls me to that same
singlehearted, exclusive devotion to Him. I think of Psalm 37:4.

My Response: Lord, thank You for being my Redeemer. I love You
with all my heart and soul.

Enriching Your Life of Prayer © 1998, 2008 Catherine Martin

Figure 4

words in Genesis 8:1: "And God remembered Noah." I listened to God that day and heard Him saying to me that He surely remembers His children. It is outside the realm of His nature to ever forget us. But I needed to hear that truth, for I was feeling forgotten, left out in the cold in my prolonged trial. God spoke, and I listened. Because I wrote down what He taught me from the Word, I can look back on that written testimony of yesterday to gain new encouragement for today and abiding hope for tomorrow. This very time of listening led to my book *Walking with the God Who Cares.*

THANK YOU, LORD: WRITE WHAT YOU ARE THANKFUL FOR

We need to thank the Lord in the midst of everything we face in life. What better way to enhance our prayer growth plan than using a Thank You, Lord page in our *Quiet Time Notebook?* (See figure 5 for an example.) You may devote a page in your journal or notebook to this aspect of your prayer growth plan. Paul encourages us to be "always giving thanks for all things in the name of our Lord Jesus Christ to God, even the Father" (Ephesians 5:20). This has become such a passion for me that it frequently becomes the primary focus for my prayers each day. "Ah," you say, "it's easy to thank the Lord each day when things go well. But what about when I am ill, lose my job, or become so depressed I cannot get out of bed?" For me, times of adversity and suffering have become opportunities to delve deep into the Word and express thankfulness to the Lord made possible only through the power of the Holy Spirit. Many times, I've discovered that God has plans that have not yet entered my mind. F.B. Meyer addresses this point: "Remember to give thanks 'always' for 'all' things. Whether you like the packing case or not, you may be sure that the contents are the very best that God could send you."[4] And many times, an entry of tears on my Thank You, Lord page has later become one of great joy and peace.

When Corrie and Betsie ten Boom arrived at Ravensbruck concentration camp during World War II, they discovered their barrack was swarming with fleas. Corrie cried out to Betsie, "How can we live in such a place?" Betsie began praying, "Show us how, show us how." Betsie turned to Corrie and asked her what they had read in the Bible that morning. She had read in 1 Thessalonians, "Give thanks in all circumstances; for this is God's will for you in Christ Jesus."

"That's it, Corrie! That's His answer. 'Give thanks in all circumstances!'... We can start right now to thank God for every single thing about this new barracks."

They started by thanking the Lord for the Bible they had been able to smuggle into the camp. Then Betsie prayed, "Thank You for the fleas and for..."

But Corrie interrupted, "Betsie, there's no way even God can make me grateful for a flea."

Betsie replied, "Fleas are part of this place where God has put us." Corrie and Betsie gave thanks for the fleas.

Sometime after this prayer, Betsie came to Corrie and said, "You know, we've never understood why we've had so much freedom in the big room. Well, I've found out." It was the fleas. The supervisors and guards refused to come through the door of their barrack because they wanted nothing to do with a place "crawling with fleas."[5]

May we learn to give thanks in all circumstances. And may we all continue to pray the prayer of the disciples, "Lord, teach us to pray."

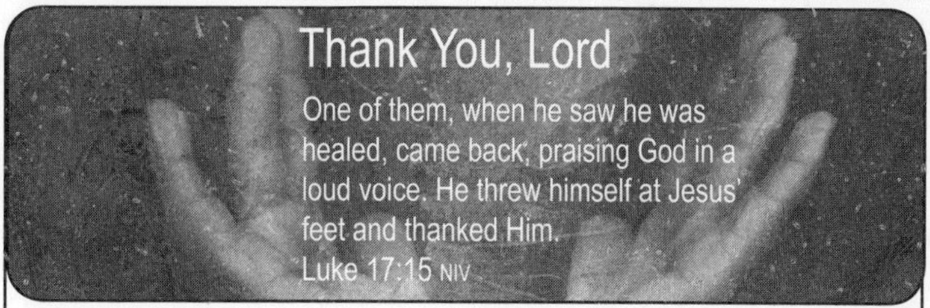

Thank You, Lord

One of them, when he saw he was healed, came back, praising God in a loud voice. He threw himself at Jesus' feet and thanked Him.
Luke 17:15 NIV

Each day, try to write at least one thing you thank God for in your life.

Date	What I'm Thankful For
3-20-08	the privilege of serving You, Lord
3-25-08	the closeness of my family
3-26-08	my husband
3-30-08	being able to serve in Quiet Time Ministries
4-3-08	an idea for a new book
4-5-08	strength for today, Lord
4-8-08	Your Word and the Holy Spirit
4-10-08	spending quiet time with You

Enriching Your Life of Prayer © 1998, 2008 Catherine Martin

Figure 5

My Response

DATE:

KEY VERSE: "Ask, and it will be given to you; seek, and you will find; knock, and it will be opened to you. For everyone who asks receives, and he who seeks finds, and to him who knocks it will be opened" (Matthew 7:7-8).

FOR FURTHER THOUGHT: What was the most important thought you had today as you read? What will you need to do in your own life to begin your prayer growth plan? What idea is most exciting to you as you engage in the journey of enriching your life of prayer?

MY RESPONSE:

Day Nine

LEARNING
FROM OTHERS

*Remember those who led you, who spoke the
word of God to you; and considering the
result of their conduct, imitate their faith.*

HEBREWS 13:7

Your life of prayer will grow exponentially when you seek out the masters of prayer and explore their rich legacy of compositions. The writer of Hebrews said, "Remember those who led you, who spoke the word of God to you; and considering the result of their conduct, imitate their faith." The Greek words translated "remember" (*mnemoneuo*) and "imitate" (*mimeomai*), when put together in the same sentence, imply following an easily remembered example. Over the years some men and women have intimately known the Word of God and become prayer warriors. Some of these masters are still living today. You may be able to hear them teach in person or through electronic media. Many others of these masters are now face-to-face with the Lord, but their knowledge and learning about prayer are available to you in the books they wrote. Look to these masters to teach you how to pray.

In developing my prayer growth plan, I decided I needed to read the best books on prayer and keep track of favorite quotes. Discipleship is scriptural, and I wanted to be discipled by the prayer warriors of the past and present. Paul encouraged Timothy to pass on what he had learned to others: "The things which you have heard from me in the presence of many witnesses, entrust these to faithful men who will be able to teach others also" (2 Timothy 2:2). I wanted to be one of those faithful who, with a teachable heart, could learn about prayer and then pass on what I was learning to others. To this end, I devote a couple of simple journal pages called Quotes on Prayer and Books on Prayer. (See figures 6 and 7 for examples.) To apply this aspect of your prayer growth plan, you can use two pages in your journal or notebook.

QUOTES ON PRAYER: WRITE YOUR FAVORITE QUOTES

Quotable sayings are pithy and easy to remember, understand, and apply to your life. One of the quotes I memorized early on in my Christian walk was by Oswald Chambers: "Prayer does not equip us for greater works. Prayer *is* the greater work." I love that quote. But, where are you going to find good quotes on prayer? You can't go wrong with the basic staples of books, conferences, and multimedia. Imagine how many quotes you could glean from a DVD course such as Biblical Exposition of Prayer by Dr. James Rosscup, websites focused on prayer such as Operation World or Waymakers, or a conference such as the Global Day of Prayer. Once you've recorded your quotes, you can return to them again and again when you need encouragement to pray.

BOOKS ON PRAYER: WRITE WHAT YOU LEARN

Once I began developing my prayer growth plan, I decided I would always have a book on prayer in my quiet time basket. What makes a good book? The writer must be committed to the Lord and to the authority of God's Word. The writer should be orthodox in teaching, that is, not known to be a false or heretical teacher. Indeed, the writer of Hebrews points out that those who lead us should speak the word of God to us (Hebrews 13:7). The writer should take you directly to the Bible, with

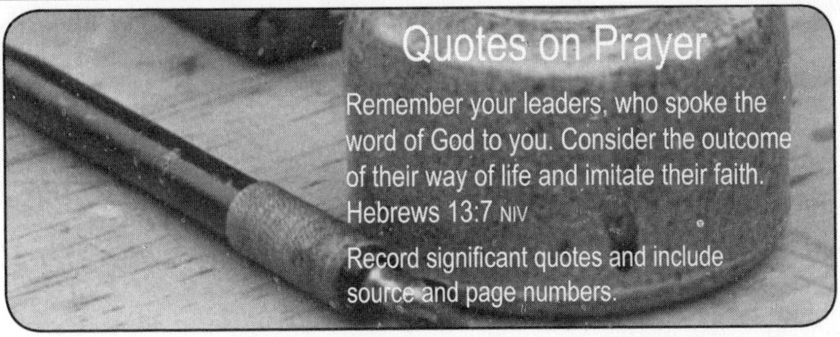

Quotes on Prayer

Remember your leaders, who spoke the word of God to you. Consider the outcome of their way of life and imitate their faith. Hebrews 13:7 NIV

Record significant quotes and include source and page numbers.

Source __With Christ in the School of Prayer__   Page(s): __16__

Jesus never taught His disciples how to preach, only how to pray. He did not speak much of what was needed to preach well, but much of praying well. To know how to speak to God is more than knowing how to speak to man. Not power with men, but power with God is the first thing. Jesus loves to teach us how to pray. Andrew Murray

Source __Quiet Talks on Prayer__   Page(s): __15__

Prayer opens a whole planet to man's activities. I can as readily be touching hearts for God in far away India or China through prayer, as though I were there...his relationship is as wide as his Master's and his sympathies should be. A man may be in Africa, but if his heart be in touch with Jesus it will be burning for a world. Prayer puts us into dynamic touch with a world. S.D. Gordon

Figure 6

Books on Prayer

Godliness has value for all things.
1 Timothy 4:8 NIV

Book: *Prayer*
Author: *Ole Hallesby*
Date Read: *3-25-08*

As you read, underline important quotes in the book you are reading on prayer and record the page number(s) and subject or quote.

Page(s)	Subject or Quote in Book
13	the breath of the soul
14	let Jesus into our needs
14	To pray is to let Jesus glorify His name in the midst of our needs.
17	in the sunshine of His grace
17	To be a Christian is in truth to have gained a place in the sun!
18	Prayer and helplessness are inseparable. Only those who are helpless can truly pray.
21	Prayer is for the helpless.
54	How God answers prayer—sending the answer
59	praying in the name of Jesus
61	the secret prayer chamber—a resting place and also a workshop

Figure 7

principles supported by Scripture itself. I am extremely selective in what I read. Time is short, and I'm not inclined to waste it on fluff or fancy. I want God's eternal perspective in everything I read. My favorite authors are A.W. Tozer, Andrew Murray, G. Campbell Morgan, Oswald Chambers, Amy Carmichael, Charles Spurgeon, and F.B. Meyer. I always want to know what God has taught them from the Bible.

You may ask, "With so many books on prayer, where do I start? Where can I begin reading about prayer?" I've included a list of recommended books on prayer in the appendix. But these are my favorites:

How to Pray by R.A. Torrey. This was the first book I read on prayer, and it is still one of my favorites. Torrey covers almost every aspect of prayer in a short amount of space, giving attention to the importance of prayer, obedience, the name of Jesus, the Holy Spirit, abiding in Christ, thanksgiving, hindrances to prayer, when to pray, and the need for revival. I highly recommend this book in your prayer arsenal. (You can read it online at www.ccel.org.)

If You Will Ask by Oswald Chambers. Oswald Chambers is another of my favorite authors and has helped me grow in my relationship with the Lord. He is one of my mentors and has discipled me over the years through his devotional *My Utmost for His Highest*. His book on prayer will challenge and teach you. He speaks about the purpose of our prayer to God:

> Prayer to Him is not a way to get things from God, but so that we may get to know God. Prayer is not to be used as the privilege of a spoiled child seeking ideal conditions to indulge his spiritual propensities; the purpose of prayer is to reveal the presence of God, equally present at all times and in every condition.

The Kneeling Christian by an unknown Christian. I have always wondered about the identity of the "unknown Christian." This book is power-packed, containing quotes and insights that will motivate you to pray.

> Unless we pray aright we cannot live aright or serve aright.

> We, His children, have the right of access to God at any time, in any place. And He understands any form of prayer. We may have a wonderful gift of speech pouring itself out in a

torrent of thanksgiving, petition, and praise like St. Paul; or we may have the quiet deep, lover-like communion of a St. John. The brilliant scholar like John Wesley and the humble cobbler like William Carey are alike welcome at the throne of grace. Influence at the court of heaven depends not upon birth, or brilliancy, or achievement, but upon humble and utter dependence upon the Son of the King.

(You can read the entire book online at www.ccel.org.)

The Power of Prayer in a Believer's Life by Charles Spurgeon. Spurgeon, the prince of preachers, was known to be a man of prayer, often talking with God even while in conversation with others around him. I will read anything by Spurgeon and own many of his books. He is one of my favorite authors because he loved the Lord, studied God's Word, thought deeply about God, knew God intimately, and enjoyed the power of the Holy Spirit in his preaching, teaching, and writing. His book on prayer will give you many secrets to enjoying a life of walking and talking with God. (For more on Spurgeon, see www.spurgeon.org.)

Power Through Prayer by E.M. Bounds. E.M. Bounds is one of the classic writers on prayer, having written at least seven books on the subject. You can read all of them at www.ccel.org. *Power Through Prayer* is known as his best and most popular work. I remember asking a friend of mine, a member of the Campus Crusade prayer ministry, what book she would recommend for me to read about prayer, and she said, "Get any book you can by E.M. Bounds. You will learn how to pray." She was right. Bounds indeed practiced what he wrote and was committed to praying even before the sun came up. He lived from 1835 to 1913 and impacted countless people in their prayer lives.

Prayer by Ole Hallesby. This book by one of Norway's leading devotional writers is full of powerful teaching on prayer. His writing makes me think, and he presents truths about prayer in new and unusual ways. For example, he speaks of prayer and helplessness. He says helplessness is our best prayer and makes us fully dependent on God.

Prayer: Finding the Heart's True Home by Richard Foster. Richard Foster's writing will help you slow down to be alone with God. He emphasizes our relationship with God and portrays truth about prayer in unusual ways. For example, he encourages you to nurture a "secret history" with the Father and develop a "familiar friendship" with Jesus. I love how he begins this book:

> Today the heart of God is an open wound of love. He aches over our distance and preoccupation. He mourns that we do not draw near to him. He grieves that we have forgotten him. He weeps over our obsession with muchness and manyness. He longs for our presence. And he is inviting you—and me— to come home, to come home to where we belong, to come home to that for which we were created. His arms are stretched out wide to receive us. His heart is enlarged to take us in.

I have read other books by Richard Foster, but in my opinion, this one on prayer is his best.

Quiet Talks on Prayer by S.D. Gordon. S.D. Gordon was a prolific author who lived from 1859 to 1936 and wrote more than 25 devotional books. Twenty-two of those books formed the Quiet Talks series. His writing was so popular that he often wrote at least two books a year. *Quiet Talks on Prayer* was the second in this series. I especially love this book for the stories and illustrations it includes. (This book is available free in e-book form at various Internet websites.)

With Christ in the School of Prayer by Andrew Murray. This book was one of the catalysts for the Welsh Revival of 1904–1905. Andrew Murray knew God, and he knew how to pray. By the time you have finished reading and meditating on the chapters of this book, you will be on fire to pray. (You can read it online at www.ccel.org.)

Your interaction with the books you read will make a difference in your prayer life and the prayer lives of others. Underline favorite quotes, write comments in the margins, and copy the quotes on your Books on Prayer notebook or journal page. When I first became a Christian, I carted around R.A. Torrey's book *How to Pray,* and I couldn't wait to share quotes from it with my friends. Before long, a lot of *How to Pray* books began flying off the shelves at the local Christian bookstore. A lot of my friends learned how to pray. And so did I. Never underestimate the power of a quote on prayer. Remember the prayer warriors and imitate their faith.

My Response

DATE:

KEY VERSE: "Remember those who led you, who spoke the word of God to you; and considering the result of their conduct, imitate their faith" (Hebrews 13:7).

FOR FURTHER THOUGHT: Look through the list of recommended books on prayer and highlight or mark in some way those books that are of most interest to you. What book will be first on your list? What is your favorite quote on prayer over the last few years? What is the most important truth or principle you've learned about prayer in the last few years?

MY RESPONSE:

Day Ten

YOUR ADVENTURE
IN PRAYER

*God himself is right alongside to keep you steady
and on track until things are all wrapped
up by Jesus. God, who got you started in
this spiritual adventure, shares with us the
life of his Son and our Master Jesus. He will
never give up on you. Never forget that.*

1 Corinthians 1:8-9 MSG

Prayer is at the very core of your great adventure of knowing God, a keystone of faith to be experienced and enjoyed until you are face-to-face with Him in paradise. You can be strongly encouraged by the words of Paul, first in the NASB and then for comparison, in the Message: "...who will also confirm you to the end, blameless in the day of our Lord Jesus Christ" is paraphrased, "God himself is right alongside you to keep you steady and on track until things are all wrapped up by Jesus." "God is faithful, through whom you were called into fellowship with His Son, Jesus Christ our Lord" is paraphrased, "God, who got you started in this spiritual adventure, shares with us the life of his Son and our Master Jesus. He will never give up on you. Never forget that" (1 Corinthians 1:8-9). The Greek word translated "confirm" is *bebaioo* and implies a blessed assurance inspiring confidence and security. How vivid a promise, how exhilarating an adventure.

I walked through the portico of the ballroom at a church, holding my breath because I was excited to greet old friends. This was a reunion gathering of our fellowship group for Campus Crusade at ASU, one I had not attended for many years. I stopped as I entered, and scanned the room, searching faces and refreshing memories. Suddenly I thought back to our times together, growing up in the Lord in those early days. About 30 of us met regularly, often at my family's home, all students beginning our relationship with the Lord. We hardly knew what prayer was, but we were eager to learn. All at once, I could see Matt leading the worship songs, Kathy reading a Bible verse, and Helen sharing from a book on prayer—and all of us with our heads bowed and our hearts aglow as we anticipated our futures. With these memories lingering in my mind, I began exchanging warm handshakes and earnest smiles, I overflowed with thanks to the Lord for teaching me to pray through these greatest of friends.

Dear friend, life is all about the great adventure of knowing God. And for me, the greatest part of that journey is passionate prayer.

In your prayer growth plan, you will want to keep track of what God is teaching you about prayer. I have discovered the great value of chronicling my adventure with the Lord. I devote a page in my *Quiet Time Notebook* to My Adventure in Prayer. (See figure 8 for an example.) I include the date, the source, what I've learned, and my response in prayer. You may apply this aspect of your prayer growth plan using your journal or a notebook. This is especially useful for examples of prayer throughout the Bible. Just recently, I was impressed with Abraham's persistent and bold prayer on behalf of Lot and his family. I learned from Abraham the importance of never giving up in prayer. I've learned from Hannah to pour out my soul to the Lord. I've learned from Nehemiah to pray on behalf of countries and God's covenant people. I've learned from Paul that I must always pray. We learn lessons quicker and remember them longer when we write them down.

My adventure in prayer has led me in some unusual directions. I never thought much about posture in prayer until my friend Jim Smoke told me he had a wooden prayer kneeler. In addition, he is big on ambience.

My Adventure in Prayer

Blessed are those whose strength is in you,
who have set their hearts on pilgrimage.
Psalm 84:5 NIV

Record your journey by writing what you are learning about prayer. Include date and key scripture/sources, and respond in prayer to God.

Date: 3-25-08
Key Verse or Source: Philippians 4:6-7
What I Am Learning:

The Lord does not want me to worry. Prayer is the prescription for worry. Peace will guard my heart like a sentry keeping out all intruders that threaten to rob me of peace.

My Response to God: Lord, I lay my worries and burdens at Your feet.

Date: 3-25-08
Key Verse or Source: S.D. Gordon in Quiet Talks on Prayer
What I Am Learning:

Prayer puts me in touch with the world. The scope of God's plan includes the world. This is powerful to me knowing that no matter what, God includes me in His plans through prayer.

My Response to God: Lord, I want to pray more for the world and specific countries in the world. Help me be more faithful in this.

Enriching Your Life of Prayer © 1998, 2008 Catherine Martin

Figure 8

He finds it helpful to turn the lights low and light a candle as he spends time with the Lord. A candle lights up the room, adds a sense of warmth and intimacy, and encourages you to remember that Jesus is the light of the world. For me, sometimes I kneel, sometimes I stand, and sometimes I am facedown on the floor. Music is another tool that sets the mood for me. I love to open my hymnbook and sing praises to the Lord. My favorite hymnbook is *Hymns for the Family of God,* and my favorite hymn is "My Jesus I Love Thee."

I have also used a prayer shawl, called a *tallit*—a garment in the Hebrew culture of praise and worship. I was exploring the Internet one day and discovered a website describing a prayer shawl and its symbolism. Four tassels, one at each of the four corners of the garment, with seven strands of white on each tassel, represent the purity and holiness of God's commandments. Woven within each white tassel is a strand of blue, representing the Messiah. In an authentic tassel on the prayer shawl, the blue dye is from snails found only in the Mediterranean. I knew that Jim Smoke had a prayer shawl that he bought when he was in Israel, so I decided to order one as well—a real, authentic prayer shawl.[1] Occasionally when I am praying, pouring out my heart to the Lord, I feel compelled to drape my prayer shawl over my head and shoulders, reminding me anew of the greatness of God and my own humility and submission to Him. I share this not to encourage outward religious affectations, but to encourage us to a deeper, more humble reverence for our great God.

We have seen the great value of personalizing prayers directly from Scripture. We can also personalize prayers written by others as long as they are scripturally based. My favorite prayers are in *The Valley of Vision: A Collection of Puritan Prayers and Devotion* edited by Arthur Bennett; *31 Days of Praise* by Ruth Myers; and *Face to Face,* volumes 1 and 2 by Kenneth Boa. The Puritan prayers are lessons in theology all by themselves. I absorb and embrace the prayers as my own and direct them to the Lord.

I've seen many amazing answers to prayer. God has specifically responded to many of my requests, some small and some large. I asked Him for computer equipment to help Quiet Time Ministries go online, and we received a donation in the exact amount needed. My friend Bev and I prayed for an assistant to join me at Quiet Time Ministries, and Kayla came to me with the news that God was leading her to join our staff. Those words from her made me cry as I realized God's specific and abundant answer to our prayers. Just recently, at the Arizona State Campus Crusade reunion, Carolyn, a former staff member, walked up to me and said, "Catherine, now I see how God has answered my prayers."

I asked, "What do you mean?"

She said, "All those years ago, while you were on staff with the Josh McDowell Ministry in Julian, California, I began praying for you, and I've never stopped. I had no idea where you were or what you were doing. But I kept praying for you. And now I see the books you've written and all God is doing in Quiet Time Ministries. God has marvelously answered my prayers in greater ways than I could have imagined." These words were so powerful and humbling as I realized someone as godly as Carolyn was faithfully praying for me even while I was unaware.

Dear friend, what is your adventure in prayer? Will you begin chronicling what God teaches you and how He answers your prayers in your journal? Will you pray to Him on your knees in a candlelit room? Will you grab a hymnbook and sing a hymn of prayer, the sun filling your face on a mountaintop? You will discover that He is "able to do immeasurably more than all we ask or imagine, according to his power that is at work within us." And you will exclaim, "To him be glory in the church and in Christ Jesus throughout all generations, for ever and ever! Amen" (Ephesians 3:20-21 NIV).

Prayer is the soul's sincere desire,
Unuttered or expressed,
The motion of a hidden fire
That trembles in the breast.
Prayer is the burden of a sigh,
The falling of a tear,
The upward glancing of the eye,
When none but God is near.
Prayer is the Christian's vital breath,
The Christian's native air,
His watchword at the gates of death;
He enters heaven with prayer.
Prayer is the contrite sinner's voice,
Returning from his ways,

While angels in their songs rejoice
And cry, "Behold, he prays!"
O Thou by whom we come to God,
The life, the truth, the way,
The path of prayer Thyself hast trod:
Lord, teach us how to pray.[2]

JAMES MONTGOMERY

DATE:

KEY VERSE: "God himself is right alongside to keep you steady and on track until things are all wrapped up by Jesus. God, who got you started in this spiritual adventure, shares with us the life of his Son and our Master Jesus. He will never give up on you. Never forget that" (1 Corinthians 1:8-9 MSG).

FOR FURTHER THOUGHT: Describe your adventure in prayer to this point in your relationship with God. What is the most important truth you've learned about prayer? Describe one important experience of answered prayer from the Lord. How will you keep track of your adventure in prayer in the next year?

MY RESPONSE:

Day Eleven

YOUR ADVENTURE
IN KNOWING GOD

The people who know their God will
display strength and take action.

DANIEL 11:32

Your greatest claim in life is that you know God. And nowhere is this claim more vividly expressed than in your life of prayer. God said, "Let him who boasts, boast of this, that he understands and knows Me" (Jeremiah 9:24). In Daniel 11:32 we see that "the people who know their God will display strength and take action." The Hebrew word translated "know" is *yada* and implies an actual experiential relationship with God, not an academic acquiring of facts. The more you know God, the more you will pray. The more intimate your relationship with Him, the more time you will spend with Him. E.M. Bounds said, "Those who know God the best are the richest and most powerful in prayer. Little acquaintance with God, and strangeness and coldness to Him, make prayer a rare and feeble thing."

At the 1992 Olympic summer games in Barcelona, Derek Redmond dreamed of winning a gold medal in the 400 meter race. He had worked hard to reach this moment. Four years earlier he had been forced to withdraw just ten minutes before competing in the 1988 games because of an Achilles tendon injury. He underwent five surgeries that next year. This was the same Derek Redmond who had shattered the British 400-meter record at the age of 19. So this was his time, his moment, his stage to do what he did best. His father, Jim, went with him to Barcelona—they were the best of friends. And he and his father agreed that regardless of what happened, he would cross the finish line.

On the day of the semifinal race, the stadium was packed with 65,000 fans. When the starter's gun went off, Derek sprang out of the starting blocks. He was positioned to advance to the finals, but suddenly, Derek heard a pop—his right hamstring. He pulled up lame, began hopping on one leg, and fell to the track. Derek's father saw tears running down his son's face, the dream of an Olympic medal shattered. But then, inside Derek, something changed. He waved off the medical crew, struggled to his feet, and slowly, one painful step at a time, started hobbling down the track. Suddenly, everyone in the stadium realized that Derek was not dropping out of the race. The crowd rose to its feet in a standing ovation that drowned out Derek's searing pain. Jim Redmond reached his son at the final curve, about 120 meters from the finish. Arm in arm, Derek and his father finished the race, just as they had vowed they would.

Like Derek Redmond, you can know that you have a Father who is not distant and uncaring, but close and accessible, and He longs to be known and loved by you. He wants an intimate, daily, moment-by-moment conversation with you. Brennan Manning, author of *The Ragamuffin Gospel*, believes that when we stand in God's presence, He will ask us this question: "Did you believe that I loved you...that I waited for you and longed to hear the sound of your voice?"[1]

As I developed my own prayer growth plan, I realized that every time I read the Bible in my quiet time, I learned something new about God. I decided that documenting my adventure in knowing God is another important component for prayer growth. So I devoted a page in my notebook to My Adventure in Knowing God. (See figure 9 for an example.)

Whenever you study the Bible, always look for truths about who God is, what God does, and what God says.[2] You will never be disappointed in this endeavor because God reveals Himself through His Word. He spoke

My Adventure in Knowing God

The name of the LORD is a strong tower; the righteous run to it and are safe.
Proverbs 18:10 NIV

The goal in prayer and in life is to know God. As you study God's Word and pray, write what you learn when God shows you a truth about Himself.

Date: 3-25-08
Key verse or source: Psalm 46:1
What I am learning about God:

I am learning that God is my refuge and my strength. He is the one I must always run to when I need help. This is particularly important and vital in my life of prayer.

My response to God: Lord, show me how to run to You as my refuge.

Date: 4-1-08
Key Verse or Source: Genesis 1:1
What I am learning about God:

I am learning more and more about God as Elohim, the Triune God, who created the heavens and the earth. What this means to me is that God can create something out of nothing, including creating something in my impossible situations. This greatly impacts and encourages my trust in God.

My response to God: Lord, thank You for creating something out of nothing, and I trust You today in my impossible situation.

Enriching Your Life of Prayer © 1998, 2008 Catherine Martin

Figure 9

the Word, and by virtue of His authorship, every Word reveals His nature. Think about that for a minute. Whenever you read any book, the writing reveals the character of the author. But the Word of God is a living, God-breathed book. Paul told Timothy, "All Scripture is God-breathed and is useful for teaching, rebuking, correcting and training in righteousness, so that the man of God may be thoroughly equipped for every good work" (2 Timothy 3:16-17 NIV). Paul's words clearly show us that God is the author of the Bible. Ask Him to show Himself to you in His Word.

When you begin looking for truths about God in the Bible, you will discover God often reveals Himself by His names. God does not have just one name, but many names. God's names are not merely identification tags, but revelations of His character. For example, when God revealed Himself to Hagar as *El Ro'i*, the God who sees, He comforted her with His abiding presence and compassionate care. Knowing God is *El Ro'i* encourages you to pray, *Lord, You are El Ro'i, the God who sees. And that means that You see me. You also see my family. And You see my daily trials. Lord, thank You that I am not alone. I trust You to be with me today and to help me make it through. Amen.*

Knowing God is *Yahweh Rophe* encourages me to pray, *Lord, You are the God who heals. And that means You can heal my friend. I pray that You will put Your healing hand on her today.*

Knowing God is *El Shaddai* encourages me to pray, *Lord, You are El Shaddai, the all-sufficient God who is everything I need for everything I face in life. Nothing is too difficult for You. I lay out my impossible situation before You now and pray that You meet the very deepest needs and accomplish Your plan and purpose.*

Every name of God offers a new approach to God, a new understanding of His nature, and a new trust in His power and might. (See appendix 2 for more prayers calling on the names of God.)

I have learned over the years that God is so much more than I thought He was or even know Him to be right now. Jeremiah found great hope in his own meditation on the greatness of God: "This I recall to mind, therefore I have hope. The LORD's lovingkindnesses indeed never cease, for His compassions never fail. They are new every morning. Great is Your faithfulness" (Lamentations 3:21-23). David found great comfort in knowing God as his shepherd (Psalm 23:1). Paul discovered the Lord as "the Father of mercies and the God of all comfort" (2 Corinthians 1:3). Peter knew God as "the Shepherd and Guardian of your souls" (1 Peter 2:25).

And now, dear friend, how well do you know your God? Will you spend time in His Word to get to know Him, and will you chronicle your journey? This week you've learned eight new ways to grow in your life of walking and talking with the Lord. I encourage you to try one new idea in your quiet time. God bless you as you continue on in the great adventure of knowing Him.

My Response

DATE:

KEY VERSE: "The people who know their God will display strength and take action" (Daniel 11:32).

FOR FURTHER THOUGHT: What is the most important truth you have ever learned about God? How has knowing Him helped make you strong and empowered you to live for Him? Will you take the time to chronicle your adventure of knowing God? Close by writing a prayer to the Lord, expressing your desire to know Him.

MY RESPONSE:

QUIET TIME
WEEK TWO:
THE PARTNERSHIP
OF PRAYER

I will not leave you as orphans; I will come to you.
JOHN 14:18

PREPARE YOUR HEART

In the last two weeks you have had the opportunity to think about the life of prayer and how you can grow deeper in walking and talking with your God. And now the question is, are you walking and talking with your Lord? Do you see that prayer does not occur in a vacuum, but in the context of an intimate relationship with the Lord? It has been said that the best way to learn to pray is to pray. Today, as you begin your quiet time, pray the prayer of Jesus' disciples: *Lord, teach me to pray.*

READ AND STUDY GOD'S WORD

1. Read John 14 and write out everything that helps you understand the intimacy of your relationship with the Lord.

2. Jesus prayed an incredible prayer for His disciples and included you in that prayer. Read John 17 and write out what is most significant to you in His prayer.

ADORE GOD IN PRAYER

My soul wakes early and turns to you, O God, for the light. Your light is better than life; therefore, my lips shall praise you. Take my hand in yours, and make the crooked places straight and the rough places plain, that your name may be glorified in my daily walk and conversation.[1]

F.B. MEYER

YIELD YOURSELF TO GOD

Jesus never sends a man ahead alone. He blazes a clear way through every thicket and woods, and then softly calls, "Follow me. Let's go on together you and I." He has been everywhere that we are called to go. His feet have trodden down smooth a path through every experience that comes to us. He knows each road and knows it well: the valley road of disappointment with its dark shadows; the steep path of temptation down through the rocky ravines and slippery gullies; the narrow path of pain, with the brambly thorn bushes so close on each side, with their slash and sting; the dizzy road along the heights of victory; the old beaten road of commonplace daily routine. Everyday paths He has trodden and glorified, and will walk anew with each of us. The only safe way to travel is with Him alongside and in control.[2]

S.D. GORDON

Roadmates

Come, share the road with Me, My own,
Through good and evil weather;
Two better speed than one alone,
So let us go together.

Come, share the road with Me, My own,
You know I'll never fail you,
And doubts and fears of the unknown
Shall never more assail you.

Come, share the road with Me, My own,
I'll share your joys and sorrows.
And hand in hand we'll see the throne
And God's great glad tomorrows.

Come, share the road with Me, My own,
And where the black clouds gather,
I'll share thy load with thee, My son,
And we'll press on together.

And as we go we'll share also
With all who travel on it,
For all who share the road with Me
Must share with all upon it.

So make we—all one company,
Love's golden cord our tether,
And, come what may, we'll climb the way
Together—aye, together![3]

JOHN OXENHAM

ENJOY HIS PRESENCE

Think carefully and honestly about your relationship with God. Are you walking and talking with Him, or do you live a life of independence? How does what you have learned about your relationship with the Lord today help you in your life of prayer? Write a prayer to the Lord, asking

Him to help you remember that life is all about the great adventure of knowing Him.

REST IN HIS LOVE

"Whatever you ask in My name, that will I do, so that the Father may be glorified in the Son. If you ask Me anything in My name, I will do it" (John 14:13-14).

Notes—Week Two

Week Three

PATTERNS FOR YOUR
LIFE OF PRAYER

Days 13–18

Day Thirteen

THE PRAYER LIFE
OF HANNAH

*She, greatly distressed, prayed to
the LORD and wept bitterly.*

1 SAMUEL 1:10

Passionate prayer to the Lord is a crucial and pivotal response in a time of distress. God is near to the brokenhearted and saves those who are crushed in spirit (Psalm 34:18). The Bible offers an example for us of one whose life of prayer flourished in her time of suffering. Hannah was greatly distressed because she was unable to bear children. Her rival, Peninnah, had children and provoked Hannah just to irritate her. Hannah's husband asked her, "Hannah, why do you weep and why do you not eat and why is your heart sad? Am I not better to you than ten sons?" (1 Samuel 1:8). What was the result for Hannah? Hannah was in great pain and distress. Her heart and soul were in anguish, mourning and loss her apparent lot in life. Hannah was helpless, with no answer for her situation and no power to do anything to change her circumstance.

Have you ever found yourself in just such a place? Without an obvious answer, seemingly without hope, without cure? What will you do? Hannah, "greatly distressed, prayed to the LORD and wept bitterly."

When you are at your wit's end and seem to be sinking in the pit of your circumstances, you need to know that you are not at the end. You are at the beginning of something new and marvelous that God has planned for you. Spurgeon says, "Man's extremity is God's opportunity." Memorize that quote; write it down so you can always remember it. When you feel as though you are at a dead end, when you think you have no way out, when you believe there is no hope—think again. There is one place yet to travel. Discover God's promises in His Word and then run with your biblical convictions to the Lord in prayer. Ole Hallesby says that your helplessness...

> is the most powerful plea which rises up to the tender father-heart of God...Your helplessness is the very thing which opens wide the door unto Him and gives Him access to all your needs...Helplessness is the real secret and impelling power of prayer...Such prayers make an impression in heaven...Our helplessness has now become the quiet, sustaining power of our prayer life. A humble and contrite heart knows that it can merit nothing before God, and that all that is necessary is to be reconciled to one's helplessness and let our holy and almighty God care for us, just as an infant surrenders itself to its mother's care. Prayer therefore consists simply in telling God day by day in what ways we feel that we are helpless.[1]

According to Scripture, Hannah's prayer was spoken in her heart—her lips were moving, but her voice was not heard by those around her. The priest in attendance thought she had been drinking. Again, Hannah was the misunderstood one. She replied, "No, my lord, I am a woman oppressed in spirit; I have drunk neither wine nor strong drink, but I have poured out my soul before the LORD" (1 Samuel 1:15). Have you learned, dear friend, to pour out your soul to the Lord when you are in distress? Pouring out your soul is the prayer of total dependence on the Lord. When you pray like Hannah, though your words may not be heard aloud, your heart is heard by God. Spurgeon also says, "Groanings which cannot be uttered are often prayers which cannot be refused."[2]

The psalmist shows us how to pour out our souls in the days when God doesn't seem to be answering our prayers:

> These things I remember and I pour out my soul within me.
> For I used to go along with the throng and lead them in procession to the house of God,
> With the voice of joy and thanksgiving, a multitude keeping festival.
> Why are you in despair, O my soul?
> And why have you become disturbed within me?
> Hope in God, for I shall again praise Him
> For the help of His presence.
> O my God, my soul is in despair within me;
> Therefore I remember You...
> All Your breakers and Your waves have rolled over me.
> The LORD will command His lovingkindness in the daytime;
> And His song will be with me in the night,
> A prayer to the God of my life (Psalm 42:4-8).

The psalmist poured out his pain to the Lord, and in doing so, he was brought to a place of promise—the promise of God's presence, His loving kindness, and His song. And that is what God does—He brings us to a deeper intimacy with Him through our suffering and helplessness.

Hannah was brought to a place of helpless surrender before her mighty God, and her prayer took her to a new place where she told the Lord that if she did receive a son from Him, she would give her son to the Lord forever. Your prayer may take you to a new place of surrender as well. Your surrender opens the way to the renewed promise of God's plans and purposes in your life. Such was the case for Hannah. Now God could carry out His powerful plan—He gave Hannah a very special son, Samuel, who became God's prophet, His spokesman for His people during the reigns of Saul and David.

Even Jesus came to this same kind of surrender in Gethsemane when He exclaimed, "Abba! Father! All things are possible for You; remove this cup from Me; yet not what I will, but what You will" (Mark 14:36). The surrender of Jesus led first to the cross and ultimately to a crown of glory for Him, and it led to forgiveness of sins and eternal life for you and me.

Spurgeon, in a sermon on trials and distress, points out the plan and purpose of God behind our most bitter sufferings. "Those people who only sail in a little boat on a lake have no stories to tell of adventures at sea. But he who is to write a book describing long voyages must travel far out of sight of land and behold the sea in the time of storm, as well as in a calm." There is to Spurgeon great value in becoming the "experienced Christian" who can bring great honor to God by comforting others because he has weathered the storm himself. Spurgeon likens our experience of trials as being "trained into a hero," and that cannot be accomplished "except by great and bitter griefs coming upon you." But Spurgeon, a man who endured both success and failure, also saw his fellow man in realistic terms. "There must be many a man who knows within himself that he cannot be trusted with success." And this is his conclusion: "God will not kill His children with sweets any more than He will destroy them with bitters." But Spurgeon is no fatalist; he is grounded in the Word. Spurgeon sees mercy in the midst of our suffering and hope at the end of the trial. "When that tonic is so bitter that they seem as if they could not drink it and live, their Lord will either take the tonic away, or give them some delicious sweetness to remove all the bitter taste."[3]

The Lord met Hannah that day in the temple when she poured out her soul to Him. He moved the priest, Eli, to speak encouraging words to Hannah. Eli is Spurgeon's "experienced believer." And oh, how Hannah needed kind words from Eli for her dark day. He said, "Go in peace; and may the God of Israel grant your petition that you have asked of Him" (1 Samuel 1:17). Those words signaled a new day for Hannah. Eli reminded Hannah of God's response to prayer. Perhaps until that moment, Hannah felt as though her prayers were not going beyond the ceiling of the temple. Regardless of how she felt, she continued to pray to the Lord and pour out her soul to Him. God honors such humility and faithfulness. He is greatly glorified when we hand over our impossible situation to Him, for "all things are possible with God" (Mark 10:27). If God is able to speak the universe into existence, He can surely make something out of the apparent "nothing" of your present circumstance. After pouring out her soul, the result for Hannah was healing and comfort for her wounded heart. As Spurgeon may have phrased it, God gave Hannah some delicious sweetness to remove the bitter taste of despair. "So the woman went her way and ate, and her face was no longer sad" (1 Samuel 1:18).

Why run to God when you are in despair and are distressed beyond measure? Because He is the only one who can touch the heart, calm the spirit, and comfort the pain. Spurgeon again says, "Here, however, is my joy. My Master can do what his servant cannot. He can make the tongue of the dumb sing. He delights to look after desperate cases. *Man's extremity becomes his opportunity.* Where the most affectionate words of ours fail, the consolations of his blessed Spirit are divinely efficacious."[4]

Learn this lesson from the prayer life of Hannah and the faith of Spurgeon—there is only one place to run when your soul is in trouble, pain, and distress—to the Lord in prayer. He will meet you in your distress and answer you in His time according to His plan and purpose for your life.

My Response

DATE:

KEY VERSE: "She, greatly distressed, prayed to the LORD and wept bitterly" (1 Samuel 1:10).

FOR FURTHER THOUGHT: What is the most important truth you learned from Hannah? How does her life of prayer encourage you today? Write a prayer to the Lord, pouring out your soul to Him.

MY RESPONSE:

Day Fourteen

THE PRAYER LIFE
OF NEHEMIAH

*When I heard these words, I sat down and
wept and mourned for days; and I was fasting
and praying before the God of heaven.*

NEHEMIAH 1:4

Discernment, a gift of wisdom and knowledge from God, is first and foremost an admonition for the purpose of prayer. When you are given discernment, you are to pray. Paul prayed for the Philippian church, that their love may abound in discernment. The Greek word translated "discernment" is *aesthesis,* implying perception with the senses as well as the mind. Secular dictionaries emphasize worldly insight combined with understanding (knowledge), but the Bible clearly emphasizes wisdom from God as the key to discernment (Proverbs 2:6-10; 9:10; Ecclesiastes 2:26). Psalm 119:66 says, "Teach me good discernment and knowledge, for I believe in Your commandments." Matthew Henry summarizes the purpose of discernment: "Many have knowledge, but little judgment...Those who have both are furnished for the service of God."[1]

Oswald Chambers proclaims, "Discernment is God's call to intercession, never to faultfinding."[2] In Ezekiel 22:29, the Lord spoke of the oppression and robbery among His people and then declared, "I searched for a man among them who would build up the wall and stand in the gap before Me for the land" (Ezekiel 22:30). What would move a man to take up that kind of immense responsibility described by God? One who has a discerning heart, seeing the people's brokenness and sin and then turning to God in prayer. God raised up just such a man who, with a discerning heart, did indeed turn to God in prayer. That man was Nehemiah, the cupbearer to King Artaxerxes.

Now some men from Judah, including Nehemiah's brother, Hanani, visited him with news about Jerusalem following the 70 years of captivity in Babylon and the return of the remnant of Jews to Jerusalem. They told Nehemiah, "The remnant there in the province who survived the captivity are in great distress and reproach, and the wall of Jerusalem is broken down and its gates are burned with fire" (Nehemiah 1:3). The news did not reach the ears of a pastor, a rabbi, or a king. Just a simple servant with a heart turned to the Lord—Nehemiah, the man whose eyes and ears were open to heaven. And Nehemiah's heart was broken: "When I heard these words, I sat down and wept and mourned for days; and I was fasting and praying before the God of heaven." Such is the response of the man or woman of God who has a discerning heart.

Nehemiah, the servant of God with wisdom and knowledge, saw what few men could see. He discerned the corrupt actions against God that led to Judah's captivity in Babylon. He saw the disobedience and lack of respect for God's Word. He realized the sins of his people were offensive to his just, righteous, and holy God. And so he wept, mourned, fasted, and prayed. When we share the heart of God, we will be broken by what breaks His heart. We will be burdened by the burdens on His heart. And we will be encouraged by what brings Him joy. Nehemiah was God's man for the desperate hour of His people. If Nehemiah would respond in prayer, step beyond his human emotions, and embrace his defining moment, he would become God's instrument in the life of those who had returned to Jerusalem.

It came to pass that Nehemiah did respond in prayer and fasting, and his brokenness led to great blessing. God is indeed near to the brokenhearted, and He saves those who are crushed in spirit (Psalm 34:18). We also know that "the LORD is near to all who call upon Him, to all who call upon Him in truth. He will fulfill the desire of those who fear Him; He will also hear their cry and will save them" (Psalm 145:18-19). Nehemiah prayed the kind of prayer we must pray when we see sin, devastation, brokenness, and unfaithfulness in the lives of those around us. He prayed a prayer of confession, prayed the promises of God in His Word, and prayed for God's powerful response in a desperate hour.

In his discerning prayer, Nehemiah saw the deep need of God's people, and became willing to play his part in God's answer to that need even if his desire seemed impossible to carry out. After all, he was in service to an earthly king. He had a full-time job. How could he possibly go to help rebuild the wall around his beloved city, Jerusalem?

The king saw the sadness on his face and asked Nehemiah, "What would you request?" (Nehemiah 2:4). How did Nehemiah respond? Did he pull out plans and flowcharts? No—he "prayed to the God of heaven." Then he told the king he wished to rebuild the wall around Jerusalem. With the king's permission, Nehemiah traveled to Jerusalem, and he relied on God for his success.

How do you know when you've been given discernment for the purpose of prayer? First you have a respect for God's Word, then your heart is broken as you see circumstances contrary to God's Word, and finally you pray with a reliance on God for success.

Dr. A.T. Pierson studied the history of revivals and spiritual awakenings, and he made this conclusion: "There has never been a spiritual awakening in any country or locality that did not begin in united prayer." Nehemiah's extraordinary prayer of fasting and crying out to God led to a powerful awakening among the remnant in Jerusalem. He joined with Ezra in leading the people in Jerusalem to fast, humble themselves before the Lord, and confess their sins to God (Nehemiah 9:1-2). They read the Word of God for a quarter a day, and they confessed and worshipped God for another quarter of a day (Nehemiah 9:3). Following this great awakening of the spiritual lives of the people, they rebuilt the wall and made provision for worship of God in the temple.

Prayer precedes revival. In 1747, noted theologian Jonathan Edwards joined a movement from Scotland called a Concert of Prayer, promoting prayer for revival. He also wrote a book entitled *A Humble Attempt to Promote*

Explicit Agreement and Visible Union of all God's People in Extraordinary Prayer for the Revival of Religion and the Advancement of Christ's Kingdom on Earth, Pursuant to Scripture Promises and Prophecies. Perhaps too long a title for the modern reader or the *New York Times* bestseller list, but it was unique in its day. People began to unite in prayer. By the late 1700s, William Carey and other theologians began the Union of Prayer in England, and in 1791, the second great awakening swept across Great Britain.

In 1794, Isaac Backus, a Baptist pastor, issued a plea for revival and for a monthly day of prayer in all churches in America. Revival swept across New England and into frontier America in the form of Sunday schools, Bible societies, and the modern missionary movement. By the mid-1800's, Jeremiah Lanphier, a retired businessman, started the Fulton Street Prayer Meeting in New York City, just blocks from where the World Trade Center once stood. More than 6000 businessmen met daily to pray for revival, and more than one million people were converted to Christ.

If prayer really does precede revival, what would happen if we followed Nehemiah's example of extraordinary prayer? What if we wept and mourned over sin—not just our own sin, but also the sins of others? What if we were willing to set aside a time to fast and draw near to God in reverence and humility? We are living in a desperate hour. The world is in turmoil. Men and women are stepping away from God and His Word into lives of worldliness and complacency. The president of one research firm said that most Americans hold few convictions about their faith and have moved away from a biblical worldview. Less than half of Americans ever read the Bible outside their time in church. I believe that the Lord is once again searching for those who, like Nehemiah, will fall on their face before Him and pray for mercy, forgiveness, and empowerment. In every generation, a few have resolved to be God's man or woman, breathe the air of heaven, and share His heart. Nehemiah was willing to be that one. And I pray you will be God's person for your generation. Now is the time to step beyond your human limitations, embrace your defining moment, and become God's instrument in the place where you live.

DATE:

KEY VERSE: "When I heard these words, I sat down and wept and mourned for days; and I was fasting and praying before the God of heaven" (Nehemiah 1:4).

FOR FURTHER THOUGHT: How does Nehemiah encourage you to pray? What have you learned from his example? What do you think breaks the heart of God today? What is your response?

MY RESPONSE:

Day Fifteen

THE PRAYER LIFE
OF DANIEL

*He continued kneeling on his knees three
times a day, praying and giving thanks before
his God, as he had been doing previously.*

Daniel 6:10

Your life of prayer is a testimony to the world of the greatness and glory of God. And your prayers gain the attention and answer of God. Imagine that you are thrust into an ungodly, idolatrous foreign culture and then chosen to live in the king's court. You are to eat the food of that culture and receive the finest education possible. Such was the situation for Daniel, a Hebrew boy of 17, who was chosen to live in the court of Nebuchadnezzar, king of Babylon.

Daniel was pressured to adopt the habits of the Babylonians, thus forsaking the law, worship, and service of the one true God. However, Daniel resolved to live wisely as a young man of conviction, and he was used by God as a witness to Babylon. Daniel's wisdom and brilliance caught the attention of the new king, Darius the Mede, and Daniel was made commissioner with great powers and responsibilities. This drew the ire of royal ministers in the kingdom who sought to attack Daniel through his habit of prayer. Daniel would never compromise his prayer life, and they knew it. The ministers convinced the king to establish a law prohibiting prayer to any god other than Darius upon penalty of death in the lions' den.

Daniel was a man of prayer. His habit was to pray on his knees at least three times a day, giving thanks to God. When Daniel heard of the prohibition on prayer to God, did he hide? Did he worship in secret? No! He threw the windows open and "continued kneeling on his knees three times a day, praying and giving thanks before his God." The jealous ministers found Daniel "making petition and supplication before his God," talking with God and asking Him for mercy. Stepping back and imagining this standoff from heaven's perspective will help us understand the absolute necessity and value of our prayers. Often, we see only the earthly or horizontal view to our challenges. But considering the vertical view from heaven strengthens us to take a stand for God. What was at stake for Daniel if he obeyed the Babylonian law prohibiting prayer to the one true God? Far more than his earthly life was on trial; his very relationship with God hung in the balance.

If you've ever had the opportunity to view Peter Paul Rubens' masterpiece *Daniel in the Lions' Den* in the National Gallery of Art in Washington DC, you will appreciate the immediate intensity of Daniel's plight. I remember seeing this massive painting for the first time not long after my husband and I were married. We both stood in silence, drinking in the monumental size of the lions whose lifelike appearance seemed to leap from the canvas. We were drawn to Daniel, whose pale moonlit flesh contrasted with the fierce power of the lions' faces! The focal point is Daniel's face, which is lifted to God in prayer.

Seeing this mural was an experience I will never forget. It comes to mind nearly every time I face an impossible trial. God sent His angel to protect Daniel "because he had trusted in his God" (Daniel 6:23). As a result, Daniel's life of prayer was a testimony to all of Babylon, and King Darius decreed that everyone in the kingdom should "fear and tremble before the God of Daniel; for He is the living God and enduring forever" (Daniel 6:26). What great glory came to God because Daniel prayed!

Daniel's bold action demonstrates the power of God at work in the midst of an evil generation. I believe Daniel challenges us to examine our life of prayer. Imagine that your life of prayer is the one on trial. If you had lived at the time of Daniel, would you have been convicted and sent into that lion's den with Daniel? If not, why not? Let us heed Daniel's life of prayer as a clarion call to the church today to get serious about walking and talking with God.

What kind of person prays "on his knees three times a day…giving thanks before his God"? Who are the Daniels of recent generations, a different breed, taking God seriously and crying out to God about everything in their lives? Who might we look to as prayer warriors and examples for our own lives? Oswald Chambers, a Scottish minister and devotional writer who came to Christ through Spurgeon, was serious about prayer. He said, "What a blessed habit I have found my prayer list. Morning by morning, it takes me via the Throne of all Grace straight to the intimate personal heart of each one mentioned here, and I know that He who is not prescribed by time and geography answers immediately."[1] Here we see Chambers' commitment to quiet time ("morning by morning"), his attention to prayer ("prayer list"), his heart for intercession ("each one mentioned here"), and his trust in God ("He…answers immediately").

Rees Howells, a Welsh coal miner, came to Christ just prior to the Welsh Revival of 1904–1905. He was profoundly affected with the move of the Holy Spirit in his country and surrendered unconditionally to the Spirit in 1906. He often read the Bible on his knees and spent 40 years praying and trusting God to meet all of his needs. His life as a prayer warrior has been recounted through his biography, *Rees Howells: Intercessor* by Norman Grubb. Howells said that in his intimate, prolonged times of prayers, he "left the world outside and had access into the presence of God. It was perfect fellowship."[2] Here we see Howell's devotion to God ("left the world outside"), his effective prayers ("access into the presence of God"), and his communion with God ("perfect fellowship").

E.M. Bounds was a prayer warrior who was called to trust God for the basic essentials of life. Trained as an attorney and later the editor of a Nashville Christian newspaper, he left his secure and prestigious position for a life of preaching, praying, and writing. He prayed for three hours in the morning, ate breakfast, and studied and wrote for the rest of the day, sometimes forgetting about dinner altogether. Although he lived most of his life in obscurity, his books on prayer have helped hundreds of thousands learn to pray. He was described by his friends as "one of the most intense eagles of God that ever penetrated the spiritual ether." Bounds described his conviction this way:

> The men and women who have done the most for God in this world have been early on their knees. When we fritter away the early morning's opportunities and freshness in pursuits other than seeking God, we will make poor headway seeking him the rest of the day. If God is not first in our thoughts and efforts in the morning, he will be in the last place in the evening.[3]

Here we see Bounds' dedication ("early on their knees"), sensibility ("seeking God"), and gift of exhortation ("if God is not first in our thoughts").

Over the course of my spiritual life, I've been motivated by the testimony of those who have gone before me to dedicate time and energy to prayer. I don't pray for three hours every day as E.M. Bounds did. My calling is to write, teach, and preach. And the rush of my responsibilities has challenged the time I give to prayer. So if you feel you are not a Daniel, an Oswald Chambers, a Rees Howells, or an E.M. Bounds, you are not alone. Neither do I. Sometimes I feel like a reluctant prayer warrior.

I once received a phone call, asking me to speak at a fundraiser for the American Heart Association. My schedule was full. But I prayed and believed this was an opportunity from the Lord, so I accepted. The challenge for me was to share my testimony in the secular arena. I wondered if I would be a Daniel in the lion's den. I prayed, *Lord, please give me the words to encourage women to set aside time for prayer each day.* And, thanks to God, the words came in a message I titled, "A Quiet Heart in a Busy World." The response was overwhelming. One woman after another came to me and shared how she was encouraged to have a life of prayer. And I learned that God can even use a reluctant prayer warrior.

The Difference

I got up early one morning and rushed right into the day;
I had so much to accomplish I didn't have time to pray.
Troubles just tumbled about me and heavier came each task.

Why doesn't God help me, I wondered, He answered, *You didn't ask.*
I tried to come into God's presence, I used all my keys at the lock,
God gently and lovingly chided, *Why, child, you didn't knock.*
I wanted to see joy and beauty, but the day toiled on gray and bleak,
I called on the Lord for the reason—He said, *You didn't seek.*
I woke up early this morning and paused before entering the day.
I had so much to accomplish that I had to take time to pray.

GRACE L. NAESSENS

My Response

DATE:

KEY VERSE: "He continued kneeling on his knees three times a day, praying and giving thanks before his God, as he had been doing previously" (Daniel 6:10).

FOR FURTHER THOUGHT: What is your most significant insight about Daniel? How will his life make a difference in how you pray?

MY RESPONSE:

Day Sixteen

THE PRAYER
LIFE OF JESUS

*But Jesus Himself would often
withdraw to lonely places to pray.*

LUKE 5:16

The greatest example for your life of prayer is Jesus. When you read through the Gospels—Matthew, Mark, Luke, and John—you cannot help but notice that Jesus' prayer life dominated His days and nights. He prayed before major events, He prayed for His disciples, He prayed on the way from one town to another, He prayed on the road to suffering, and He even prayed while on the cross. He shows you what to do when you face temptation—pray. He shows you what to do when popularity and success are yours—pray. He shows you what to do when you face big decisions— pray. And He shows you how to use your time wisely—pray. Luke tells us that "the news about Him was spreading even farther, and large crowds were gathering to hear Him and to be healed of their sicknesses. But Jesus Himself would often slip away to the wilderness and pray." We see in Jesus the habit of constant prayer—an ongoing conversation, walking and talking with the Father.

Jesus' life of prayer should prompt one overwhelming prayer from us just as it did from His disciples: *Lord, teach us to pray.* Andrew Murray says, "True prayer, that takes hold of God's strength, that availeth much, to which the gates of heaven are really opened wide—who would not cry, 'Oh, for someone to teach me thus to pray'?" He concludes, "Jesus has opened a school, in which He trains His redeemed ones, who specially desire it, to have power in prayer."[1] In the university of prayer, Jesus teaches you many lessons on prayer:

Pray for everyone, even enemies (Matthew 5:44).

Prayer is an intimate conversation between you and your Father (Matthew 6:6).

Prayer should be the foundation of missions and evangelism (Matthew 9:38).

Some difficulties are overcome only through prayer and fasting (Matthew 17:21).

Prayer helps you stand strong spiritually and not give in to the flesh (Matthew 26:41).

Prayer must be accompanied by faith (Mark 11:24).

Real prayer must not bear grudges, but instead forgive (Mark 11:25).

Prayer is asking, seeking, and knocking (Luke 11:9).

Pray for what is on your heart, knowing that God will give only what is good to you, His child (Matthew 7:11; Luke 11:13).

You should always pray (Luke 18:1).

Prayer is the alternative to despair (Luke 18:1).

Prayer should be accomplished with an attitude of alertness (Luke 21:36).

Prayer makes you strong spiritually (Luke 21:36).

You can be confident that God hears your prayers (John 11:42).

Jesus teaches a methodology of prayer in the Lord's Prayer (Matthew 6:9-13). This prayer is indeed Jesus' instruction on prayer, an up close and personal how-to course for His disciples. He says, "Pray, then, in this way." The Greek word translated "in this way" is *houto* and means "after this manner," but it can be expressed as "exactly." Most scholars agree the Lord's Prayer is a model of instruction teaching us how to pray.[2] As if to punctuate this point, Jesus precedes His prayer by saying, "When you are praying, do not use meaningless repetition." I see nothing in Scripture that prohibits praying this prayer exactly, as long as it does not become "meaningless repetition." One by one, Jesus reveals the essential elements of prayer:

Our Father who is in heaven, hallowed be Your name. Begin with worship of God and ask for the advancement of the Lord's honor and the holiness of His name among men and women. In this element of prayer, you can focus on the various names of God and revere God for who He is, what He does, and what He says.

Your kingdom come. Pray for the reign and rule of God in your life and in the lives of others, asking for His kingdom to come "more and more completely until its full and final consummation."[3]

Your will be done on earth as it is in heaven. Acknowledge, submit to, and surrender to His sovereign control over the affairs of earth and heaven and over your life as well. This prayer asks for the power to say yes to God in obedience to whatever He may ask of you and to "sanctify Christ as Lord in your hearts" (1 Peter 3:15).

Give us this day our daily bread. Tell God everything you need and ask for His provision for all your life necessities. Lay out all the requests on your heart for everything you need.

And forgive us our debts, as we also have forgiven our debtors. Confess your sins to God, ask Him to show you any areas of hardness in your own heart, and then ask for the ability to forgive others who wrong you.

And do not lead us into temptation, but deliver us from evil. Ask for help in your adversity, deliverance from trials and temptations, deliverance from enemies, and strength in spiritual warfare (see Ephesians 6:10-18).

For Yours is the kingdom and the power and the glory forever. Amen. This is a doxology found in later manuscripts. Praise God for who He is, what He does, and what He says.

The Lord's prayer provides a wonderful pattern for prayer. His prayer includes worship, confession, petitions (requests), forgiveness, supplication and intercession, and praise. Sometimes I will literally pray through each phrase of the Lord's prayer and stop between each statement and amplify it with my own words of praise, worship, confession, and requests.

ACTS is a helpful acrostic incorporating elements taught in the Lord's prayer:

Adoration. I worship and praise God for who He is, what He does, and what He says.

Confession. I confess my sins to the Lord.

Thanksgiving. I thank the Lord for the blessings in my life.

Supplication. I present my requests before the Lord.

You may base your prayers on Scripture or use your own words for adoration, confession, thanksgiving, and supplication (ACTS). (See figure 10 for examples).

I have learned four important principles from the prayer life of Jesus. First, you can ask the Father *why* when you feel troubled and forsaken by God. When Jesus was hanging on the cross and darkness filled the land, He cried out with a loud voice, "My God, my God, why have You forsaken me" (Matthew 27:47). When we are face-to-face with our Lord, we will understand the depth of this prayer. But here is what we know now—Jesus prayed it, and we may also. Jesus is our great example in life. Paul tells us that we are to be like Jesus, conforming to His very image and adopting His attitude (Romans 8:29; Philippians 2:5-9). Jesus' humility, most fully seen on the cross, is the attitude we should adopt in our prayers. In complete submission to your Father, you may cry out *why* when circumstances seem to make no sense. This *why* is a cry of faith to your Father, who knows all things. Some will discourage you from asking *why*, believing such a prayer to be proud and presumptuous. However, Jesus shows us how to ask *why*: not as a demand, but as a prayer of submission. In the depth of your pain, you may become utterly poured out and emptied, with nothing left of yourself. Just crying out *why* lays your heart in the hands of your Lord.

I've also learned I may ask the Father to remove my cup of suffering. In Gethsemane, prior to His arrest, Jesus fell to the ground and prayed, "Abba!

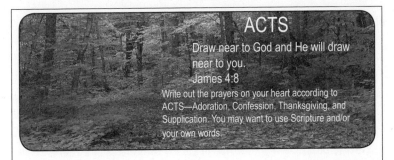

Date—Month, Week, or Day
3-25-08

Adoration
I love You, Lord, You are my strength. You are my rock, my
fortress, my protection. You are my place of safety. Psalm 18:1-2

Confession
Have mercy on me, O God, because of Your unfailing love...Wash
me clean...purify me...Create in me a clean heart... Psalm 51

Thanksgiving
You have turned my mourning into dancing. Lord, You have
clothed me with joy. I will give You thanks forever! Psalm 30:11-12

Supplication
Lord, I pray that You will deliver me and free me from all my fears.
Psalm 34:4

Date—Month, Week, or Day
4-15-08

Adoration
Lord, You are faithful and compassionate and merciful. I praise
You that You are the God of details, who loves even me.

Confession
Lord, I confess my unbelief and my habit of worrying. Help my
unbelief, dear Lord.

Thanksgiving
Lord, thank You for loving me and for guiding me, especially in
these days of uncertainty in my own life.

Supplication
Lord, make me a woman of faith who believes what You say, no
matter what.

Figure 10

Father! All things are possible for You; remove this cup from Me; yet not what I will, but what You will" (Mark 14:36). Jesus knew that His Father could do anything and asked Him to remove the suffering. However, Jesus' greater desire is seen in the word *yet*. Jesus' faith was a desperate faith, not a despairing faith. A desperate faith always desires God's plan, God's purpose, and God's will. And so Jesus prayed, "Yet not what I will, but what You will." You may ask God to take away your pain and suffering, but never forget to add the *yet* phrase. For then you will see the fulfillment of God's great plan and purpose in the light of your present difficulty.

I've also learned that prayer is more than a simple request. When the disciples asked Jesus why they had been unable to heal a demon-possessed boy, Jesus responded, "This kind cannot come out by anything but prayer" (Mark 9:29). Scripture does not record whether Jesus prayed immediately prior to healing the boy. But we do know He prayed intensely the day before at the transfiguration (Matthew 17:1; Luke 9:28-29). This was the critical point of Christ's response to the disciples. Prayer is first and foremost an intimate, ongoing relationship with God that is nurtured through specific times alone with Him. This definition has helped me understand the scope of prayer and its context in relation to the Lord. No wonder Jesus associates answers to prayer with abiding in Him (John 15:7).

And finally, Jesus shows me that prayer is essential to my life. If prayer was essential to Jesus' life, it's essential to mine. The writer of Hebrews says, "In the days of His flesh, He [Jesus] offered up both prayers and supplications with loud crying and tears to the One able to save Him from death, and He was heard because of His piety" (Hebrews 5:7). The Greek word translated "piety" is *eulabela* and also refers to reverence or devotion to God. Jesus was heard because of His devotion and reverence, expressed in His prayers as loud crying and tears. In the Greek, prayers are understood idiomatically as speaking to the Father with an open heart or from the insides.[4] Jesus prayed often, communing with the Father early in the morning (Mark 1:35), all night long (Luke 6:12), and in Gethsemane (Luke 22:39-46). If prayer was that important to Jesus, it must be absolutely essential for me. Jesus' prayer life has been the primary motivation for me to establish a daily quiet time (see Matthew 14:23; Mark 1:35; 6:46; Luke 5:16; 6:12; 9:28; John 6:15).

E.M. Bounds says this about Jesus' example:

The praying of Christ was real...Prayer pressed upon Him as a solemn, all-imperative, all-commanding duty, as well as a royal privilege...alluring and absorbing. Prayer was the secret of His power, the law of His life, the inspiration of His toil, and the source of His wealth, His joy, His communion and strength. To Christ Jesus, prayer occupied no secondary place, but was exacting and paramount, a necessity, a life, the satisfying of a restless yearning, and a preparation for heavy responsibilities... Closeting with His Father in council and fellowship, with vigour and indeed joy, all this was His praying. Present trials, future glory, the history of His Church, and the struggles and perils of His disciples in all times and to the very end of time— all these things were born and shaped by His praying. Nothing is more conspicuous in the life of our Lord than prayer.[5]

May the same be true of us. May nothing be more conspicuous in our lives than prayer.

My Response

DATE:

KEY VERSE: "But Jesus Himself would often withdraw to lonely places to pray" (Luke 5:16).

FOR FURTHER THOUGHT: How does the example of Jesus encourage you in your life of prayer? What is your favorite quote or verse from your reading today?

MY RESPONSE:

Day Seventeen

THE PRAYER LIFE OF PAUL

Pray without ceasing; in everything give thanks.
1 THESSALONIANS 5:17-18

God's will for you in Christ Jesus is to live in a continual attitude of prayer. Think of the Pauline ideal of prayer as an ongoing, unceasing conversation with your Lord, a dialogue possible even for the busiest people. Paul is your archetype, your shining example of how to pray when life is bustling, energetic, even frenzied. In three simple words, Paul presents a wealth of instruction for prayer: "Pray without ceasing." There is no hidden nuance here. The Lord is explicitly exhorting you and me to never stop praying. The Greek word translated "without ceasing" is *adialeiptos* and means "permanent" or "without intermission." He desires our company every moment of the day. If Paul, as busy as he was, could live a life of continual prayer, we can too. We soon recognize that every moment is filled with responses to God—obedience, love, submission, surrender, forgiveness, exhortation, service—all of these attitudes and activities form our life of prayer. Then prayer becomes more than just words—it becomes a lifestyle. We are praying without ceasing.

Paul's prayers will revive and reform your life of prayer. His capacity for believing God for extraordinary works is remarkable in itself. Paul's trust in God and his service among the churches cost him time, energy, comfort, and safety. He describes his life experiences to the church at Corinth as "lashes, beatings with rods, a stoning, shipwrecks, frequent travels, dangers, hard work, sleepless nights, hunger, and thirst" (2 Corinthians 11:24-28). He concludes this graphic description of suffering by admitting, "Apart from such external things, there is the daily pressure on me of concern for all the churches." So Paul's greatest suffering arose out of his love for those in the church. Paul was burdened for people—their spiritual growth and their commitment to Christ. His many letters to the churches were flooded with heartfelt prayers. Be inventive. Use Paul's words as models for your own prayers, personalizing them for others:

Romans 15:30

2 Corinthians 13:7

Ephesians 1:15-19; 3:14-21

Philippians 1:3-6

Colossians 1:3-12; 4:3

1 Thessalonians 1:2; 3:11-13

2 Thessalonians 1:3-12; 3:1-5

1 Timothy 2:1-4

Philemon 4-6

PAUL'S PRAYERS

Paul teaches you to thank God for your brethren—those who love the Lord, grow spiritually, and stand strong. Ask the Lord to increase the numbers of such men and women of God, for they are the ones He can use for the sake of the gospel. Paul said, "We ought always to give thanks to God for you, brethren...for your perseverance and faith in the midst of all your persecutions and afflictions which you endure" (2 Thessalonians 1:3-4 NIV). When you offer thanks to God, mention by name those in your life who are faithful to the Lord and living for Him. Such thanksgiving acknowledges God accomplishing a great and mighty work in the hearts of men and women.

Pray that others will live a God-honoring and God-glorifying life. Paul, throughout his prayers, considered how others lived their lives. He prayed for those in Corinth to "do no wrong" (2 Corinthians 13:7), for the Philippians to "approve the things that are excellent, in order to be sincere and blameless until the day of Christ" (Philippians 1:10), for those in Colossae to "walk in a manner worthy of the Lord, to please Him in all respects" (Colossians 1:10), and for those in Thessalonica to be "considered worthy of the kingdom of God" (2 Thessalonians 1:5). How we live our lives speaks volumes to the world. When we live a life of faith, we influence others—even after we die, according to the writer of Hebrews. Such was the case for Abel: "Though he is dead, he still speaks" (Hebrews 11:4).

Pray for others to experience the love of God in their lives. Paul asked that the Ephesians would "be able to comprehend with all the saints what is the breadth and length and height and depth, and to know the love of Christ which surpasses knowledge" (Ephesians 3:18-19). He prayed that the Thessalonians would "increase and abound in love for one another" (1 Thessalonians 3:12). He asked that the Lord would direct the hearts of those in Thessalonica "into the love of God and into the steadfastness of Christ" (2 Thessalonians 3:5). The love of God is a recurring theme in Paul's epistles.

Pray for others to see, know, and live out God's eternal perspective. Paul asked for wisdom, revelation, and enlightening of the eyes of the heart for those in Ephesus (Ephesians 1:17-18). He asked God to give the Colossians a "knowledge of His will in all spiritual wisdom and understanding" (Colossians 1:9). An eternal perspective leads to an abiding faith.

Pray for God's power to work in the lives of others through the indwelling Holy Spirit. Paul prayed for the Ephesians to know the "surpassing greatness of His power toward us who believe" (Ephesians 1:19). He also spoke of the "power that works within us" and God's ability to do "far more abundantly beyond all that we ask or think" (Ephesians 3:20).

PAUL'S THEOLOGY

Paul teaches us that God responds to our prayers with His plans. God said no to Paul's prayers to remove his thorn in the flesh (2 Corinthians 12:7). The Lord responded, "My grace is sufficient for you, for power is perfected in weakness." When we pray, God responds to us that His ways are higher than our ways (Isaiah 55:8-9). Our view is that strength is possible only when we are strong. God's view is that His strength is greatest when we are weak. When God says no to our request, He is saying yes to His higher and greater plan. At this point, we must modify our requests to our new understanding of God's desires and delights. Such heaven-touched prayers lead us into the realm of His eternal perspective.

Through his written exhortations to the churches, Paul provides a wealth of resources for our daily prayers. For example, he exhorted the Philippians to be careful about their thought life (Philippians 4:8). Using his words, you might pray, *Lord, help me to think only on those things that are true, honorable, right, pure, lovely, of good repute, excellent, and worthy of praise.* Paul exhorted the Colossians to be mindful of their priorities (Colossians 3:1-2). Using his words to the Colossians, you may pray, *Lord, I seek You, and all things that are above, with You, seated at the right hand of God. Lord, help me to set my mind on those things above, not on the things that are on the earth.* And Paul exhorted the Ephesians to be controlled and empowered by the Holy Spirit (Ephesians 5:18). Your prayer, day by day, can be *Lord, fill me with Your Holy Spirit.*

Paul has helped me understand how to aspire to a life that will honor the Lord. He encourages me to pray that I will "do all things for the sake of the gospel" (1 Corinthians 9:23), "run in such a way that I may win" (1 Corinthians 9:24), and reach for "the prize of the upward call of God in Christ Jesus" (Philippians 3:14). He has shown me that the greatest ambition I can have is to know the Lord Jesus Christ (Philippians 3:8). But the world would have you aspire to the Humanist Manifesto, which discounts belief in any personal deity or higher power. To the humanist, knowledge is derived from rational analysis and not God, humans result from unguided evolutionary change and not creation, and life's fulfillment emerges in the service of humane ideals and not the will of God. The notable signatories on the Humanist Manifesto are a veritable who's who of university presidents, well-known politicians, gifted scientists, and Nobel laureates. But for me, I prefer to listen to God's voice in the apostle Paul's advice and to adopt Paul's aspirations: "For to me, to live is Christ" (Philippians 1:21).

Paul's words fuel my prayers. One of God's best promises was written by Paul to the Philippians: "And my God will supply all your needs according to His riches in glory in Christ Jesus" (Philippians 4:19). I count on this promise for God's provision, and so do many others. Dr. Helen Roseveare, a medical missionary for 20 years in the former Belgian Congo, tells the story of a little girl's prayer: "One night I had worked hard to help a mother in the labor ward; but in spite of all we could do, she died, leaving us with a tiny premature baby, and a crying two-year-old daughter." Without an incubator or special feeding facilities, keeping the baby alive would be nearly impossible. Even in a tropical climate, the nights could be very cold with treacherous drafts. And what was worse, the last hot water bottle had burst. Hot water bottles "do not grow on trees, and there are no drugstores down forest pathways."

Dr. Roseveare instructed the student midwife, "Put the baby as near the fire as you safely can; sleep between the baby and the door to keep it free from drafts. Your job is to keep the baby warm." The next day, Dr. Roseveare went to have prayers with the orphanage children as she often did. She gave the children some things to pray about and told them of the plight of the premature baby and her orphaned sister. During their prayer time, one ten-year-old girl named Ruth prayed, *Please, God, send us a water bottle. It'll be no good tomorrow, God, as the baby'll be dead, so please send it this afternoon.* And then as an afterthought, *And while You are about it, would You please send a dolly for the little girl so she'll know You really love her?*

Dr. Roseveare wrestled with the bluntness of this young girl's prayers. "I just did not believe that God could do this. Oh, yes, I know that He can do everything. The Bible says so. But there are limits, aren't there?" Later that day, on her front porch, a 22-pound parcel arrived from home, the first such parcel in four years. With tears rolling down her face, she called for the children from the orphanage to help her open the box. Their eyes widened as Dr. Roseveare pulled out brightly colored shirts from the top of the box. Then knitted bandages for leprosy patients. And then, as she reached deeper into the box, she could hardly believe what she felt. "Could it be? Yes, a brand-new rubber hot water bottle!"

Ruth rushed forward, "If God has sent the bottle, He must have sent the dolly, too!" Ruth reached to the bottom of the box and pulled out the most beautifully dressed doll. Her eyes were bright with excitement as she asked, "Can I go over with you, Mummy, and give this dolly to that little girl, so she'll know that Jesus really loves her?" Dr. Roseveare never forgot God's provision, sent five months in advance but arriving by God's design just in time in answer to a little girl's believing prayer.

Even though I have days when I am discouraged, I turn to the words of Paul to fuel my prayers. He lifts my sights beyond the things of this world. Regardless of how difficult the particular challenge, I can turn to the words of Paul in Colossians. He reminds me to set my mind on things above, not on the things that are on earth (Colossians 3:2). And that is what we must do in times of discouragement and despair. We can grab on to God's Word, pray His Word, and lift our sights from earth to heaven.

What would I do without Paul's influence in my life? I am most encouraged when I realize that Paul's God is my Lord as well. D.A. Carson, professor of New Testament at Trinity Evangelical Divinity School, explains, "I do not know the end from the beginning. Only God does. But he is interested in me as his child, in the same way that he was interested in the life and ministry of the apostle Paul."[1] God not only longed for Paul's company, He longs for mine. He not only listened to Paul's prayers, He listens to mine. He not only wanted Paul's service, He wants mine. And dear friend, Carson speaks my heart as well when he concludes, "Just as God's unexpected answer to Paul's prayers was his best possible answer…so also his answers to our prayers will always be for his glory and his people's good."[2] May we follow Paul's example during our brief stay on earth; may we pray about everything all the time.

My Response

DATE:

KEY VERSE: "Pray without ceasing" (1 Thessalonians 5:17).

FOR FURTHER THOUGHT: How has Paul changed your view of prayer? What have you learned from his example that will help you in your own life of prayer?

MY RESPONSE:

QUIET TIME WEEK THREE: THE PRIVACY OF PRAYER

But you, when you pray, go into your inner room, close your door and pray to your Father who is in secret, and your Father who sees what is done in secret will reward you.

MATTHEW 6:6

PREPARE YOUR HEART

Lyle Dorsett described E.M. Bounds as a "man of prayer." How did Dorsett know Bounds was a man of prayer? Very little is actually known about the life of Bounds except one overwhelming passion—prayer. He wrote a few books on theological topics, but he wrote eight books on prayer. The books on prayer, especially *Power Through Prayer,* have endured to this day and have motivated thousands to set aside time in their busy schedules and pray. The prayer life Bounds wrote about for the public was exemplified in the company he kept with his Lord in private. He daily communed with God for hours. His life spoke of the private hours with the Lord, for people cannot speak for very long about what they do not know.

Bounds was invited by Homer Hodge, a pastor in Atlanta, to speak at a ministerial conference. Bounds spoke for eight days on one subject—prayer. Hodge was so impressed by his example of prayer that he asked Bounds to disciple him over the next eight years.

The time you spend with God in private will make you who you are in public. As you begin your time with the Lord today, ask Him to show you the importance of setting aside time in private for a life of prayer with Him.

READ AND STUDY GOD'S WORD

1. Jesus spoke of prayer in a new way when He taught. The Pharisees were known for the many words in their public prayers. Jesus taught the true nature of prayer in the audience of God. Read Matthew 6:1-8 and write out what you learn about how to pray.

2. Jesus modeled a private, personal life of prayer for His disciples. Look at the following verses and record what you learn about Jesus' life of prayer:

Matthew 14:21-23

Mark 1:32-35

Luke 5:15-16

Luke 6:11-13

ADORE GOD IN PRAYER

The Golden Cord

Through every minute of this day,
Be with me, Lord!
Through every day of all this week,
Be with me, Lord!
Through every week of all this year,
Be with me, Lord!
Through all the years of all this life,
Be with me, Lord!
So shall the days and weeks and years
Be threaded on a golden cord,
And all draw on with sweet accord
Unto Thy fulness, Lord,
That so, when time is past,
By Grace, I may at last,
Be with Thee, Lord.[1]

JOHN OXENHAM

YIELD YOURSELF TO GOD

Prayer wonderfully clears the vision; steadies the nerves; defines duty; stiffens the purpose; sweetens and strengthens the spirit. The busier the day for Him the more surely must the morning appointment be kept, and even an earlier start made, apparently. The more virtue went forth from Him, the more certainly must He spend time, and even more time, alone with Him who is the source of power…being compelled by the greatness of the crowds to go into the deserts or country districts, and being constantly thronged there by the people, He had less opportunity to get alone, and yet more need, and so while He patiently continues His work among them He studiously seeks opportunity to retire at intervals from the crowds to pray.

How much His life was like ours. Pressed by duties, by opportunities for service, by the great need around us, we are strongly tempted to give less time to the inner chamber, with the door shut. "Surely this work must be done," we think, "though it does crowd and flurry our prayer time some." "No," the Master's practice here says with intense emphasis. Not work first, and prayer to bless it. But the first place given to prayer and then the service growing out of such prayer will be charged with unmeasured power. The greater the outer pressure on His closet-life, the more jealously He guarded against either a shortening of its time or a flurrying of its spirit. The tighter the tension, the more time must there be for unhurried prayer.

He knew where to find rest, and sweet fellowship, and a calming presence, and wise counsel. Turning His face northward He sought the solitude of the mountain not far off for quiet meditation and prayer…And still He prayed, while the darkness below and the blue above deepened, and the stilling calm of God wrapped all nature around, and hushed His heart into a deeper peace. In the fascination of the Father's loving presence He was utterly lost to the flight of time.[2]

S.D. Gordon

Enjoy His Presence

Robert Murray McCheyne said, "What a man is alone on his knees before God, that he is, and no more."[3] Dear friend, do you know this private life of prayer spoken of by McCheyne and modeled by your Lord? If a private life of prayer was important to Jesus, then the prayer closet is imperative in your life. Jesus' attitude about His morning time is reflected in Isaiah 50:4-5: "The Lord God has given Me the tongue of disciples, that I may know how to sustain the weary one with a word. He awakens Me morning by morning, He awakens My ear to listen as a disciple. The Lord God has opened My ear; and I was not disobedient nor did I turn back." Your life of prayer is the secret to faithful service to God, wisdom in ministry, and power in living. Will you serve the Lord Jesus, first and foremost, through prayer "in the closet," with a rich and full interior life? Frederick William Faber says that nothing is so beautiful as those who serve Jesus out of love, "in the wear and tear of common, unpoetic life."[4] Close your time today by writing a prayer to your Lord, asking Him to help you develop a daily life of communing with Him in private prayer. Always remember His promise: "Your Father who sees what is done in secret will reward you" (Matthew 6:6).

Rest in His Love

"In the early morning, while it was still dark, Jesus got up, left the house, and went away to a secluded place, and was praying there" (Mark 1:35).

Notes—Week Three

PROMISES FOR YOUR
LIFE OF PRAYER

Days 19–24

Day Nineteen

THE GREAT RESPONSE OF GOD

The righteous cry, and the LORD hears and
delivers them out of all their troubles.

PSALM 34:17

When you join your passionate prayers with God's steadfast promises, you enter into the sacred land of hope. For every promise from God encourages you of His answer, His response. God's responses run in tandem with His promises. He never acts outside of the realm of His character, His deeds, or His Word. He is who He is. He does what He does. And He says what He says.

Over the next five days, we are going to focus on five powerful promises for you to carry in your prayers and on into the throne room of God. When you attach your prayers to God's promises, you can know that each promise is personally endorsed by God Himself, for He is the author of His Word. If you ever want to understand what God desires to do, turn to His promises. His promises will fill you with confidence, for they help you pray according to His will. In 1 John 5:14-15, we learn that "this is the confidence which we have before Him, that, if we ask anything according to His will, He hears us. And if we know that He hears us in whatever we ask, we know that we have the requests which we have asked from Him."

Claiming God's promises never means telling God what He is going to do. In fact, embracing God's promise often means a surrender of your own ideas of what God will do, laying out your own desires, trusting Him, and watching eagerly to see what He is going to do.[1] Prayer is not attempting to bend God to condescend to our wishings and wantings. Instead, we grasp hold of His desires, gain insight into His will, experience His plans and purposes, and ultimately see His glory accomplished for all eternity.

Prayer brings relief and comfort in times of trouble when you need deliverance. The Hebrew word translated "delivers" in Psalm 34:17 is *natsal* and means to save or rescue. As a child, when I encountered difficulties of any magnitude, small or large, the first person I ran to was my parent. And so it is with you. When you are in trouble, the first one you must run to is your heavenly Father. Jesus and Paul both cry out, "Abba! Father!" The Aramaic word could be translated "Papa" or "Daddy," implying a most precious and affectionate relationship with God. Have you learned, in the midst of your difficulties, to cry out to the Lord?

David, the shepherd boy, giant slayer, and eventual king of Israel, had learned this secret of running to the Father in the early days of his life of prayer. When he wrote Psalm 37, that secret was being put to a new test. King Saul discovered that he had lost God's favor and that God was going to take the throne from him and give it to someone else (1 Samuel 15:23-28). Saul was jealous of David, knowing that David enjoyed the favor and smile of God. The Bible tells us that the Spirit came mightily upon David and that David was God's choice for king (1 Samuel 16:12-13). Thus began the end of Saul's reign; Saul determined in his heart to kill David. Once David realized he was in danger, he fled, hiding in caves and even venturing into enemy territory to escape. Imagine David's distress and anxiety as he was being chased by the king. On one occasion, David sought refuge from Achish (Abimelech), the king of Gath. But David's sense of safety was short-lived, for Achish recognized David and knew he was running from Saul. The text tells us that "David took these words to heart and greatly feared Achish king of Gath" (1 Samuel 21:12). David wisely feigned insanity before Achish and escaped, departing from there and hiding in the cave of Adullam (1 Samuel 22:1).

Sometimes when we read historical passages in the Bible, we forget that these are not simply stories, but real-life events with real-life people. God often gives us glimpses into the hearts and minds of His people to show us spiritual secrets—truths from the Bible to help us in our own relationship with God. In this particular event in the life of David, we receive an insightful look at David's spiritual life through his journal writing in Psalm 34. Scholars believe that David wrote this psalm while facing the imminent and very real danger of the king of Gath. One dominant action is evident throughout Psalm 34: David cried out to the Lord. And when he did, the Lord heard and responded. David explains, "This poor man cried, and the LORD heard him and saved him out of all his troubles." Again David tells us, "The eyes of the LORD are toward the righteous and His ears are open to their cry." And finally, he says, "The righteous cry, and the LORD hears and delivers them out of all their troubles." David's attitude in Psalm 34 is not one of denial, despair, or defeat! David was sometimes brokenhearted and crushed in spirit, but he feared the Lord and was delivered.

What lesson can you learn from David today? When you are in need, cry out to the Lord. Take your troubles to the one who has the power and strength to meet you in your deepest need. Run to God first, not last. He is always your first help, not only your final hope. Even Paul told his disciple Timothy, "The first thing I want you to do is pray" (1 Timothy 2:1 MSG).

In the heat of the battle, you might easily overlook the truth from God's Word that God has a plan in the midst of your trial. May His plan and purpose motivate you to cry out to Him. When all seems lost, you can know you are never without hope. In Psalm 34, David exclaimed, "I sought the LORD, and He answered me, and delivered me from all my fears…to those who fear Him, there is no want…The LORD redeems the soul of His servants." When all seems over, you can know God is not worried or wondering what He is going to do. How often we act as though God is powerless to deal with those things that have brought us such pain. But you, having discovered the power of walking and talking with God, can know that "God causes everything to work together for the good of those who love God and are called according to His purpose for them" (Romans 8:28 NLT).

The story is told that in the famous lace shops of Brussels, certain rooms are devoted to weaving the most delicate and intricate patterns. These rooms are kept completely dark except for the single light focused directly on the pattern. How does darkness contribute to the design? "Lace is always more delicately and beautifully woven when the worker himself is in the dark and only his pattern is in the light."[2] And so it is with you. One day you will see that the dark periods of your life were the stage for the most exquisite weaving patterned by God Himself.

In the turbulence of a trial you will discover in new ways that God is more powerful than your trouble. Was it not so for Moses in the wilderness, and Paul in prison? Then why not for you? No wonder Paul, an expert on suffering and sacrifice, could declare, "But in all these things we have full victory through God who showed his love for us" (Romans 8:37 NCV). Our God is the God of deliverances—He is the God who helps us every day and saves us (Psalm 68:19-20). And so, what must you do? Cry out to God. Be careful never to waste a moment running to worldly solutions—run to God first. And hold on to the promise from David in Psalm 34:17 that when the righteous cry, the Lord hears, and He delivers.

Hide God's response to your cries in your heart! He hears and delivers. I love pondering God's rescue and deliverance. "But in my distress I cried out to the LORD, yes, I prayed to my God for help. He heard me from his sanctuary; my cry to him reached his ears. Then the earth quaked and trembled. The foundations of the mountains shook; they quaked because of his anger…He opened the heavens and came down…He reached down from heaven and rescued me; he drew me out of deep waters" (Psalm 18:6-16 NLT). When David speaks in such descriptive language, you can more vividly understand the champion heart of your God, His desire to deliver, and His power to save you. I encourage you to pray often when you are in trouble.

Sometimes my own troubles become overwhelming to me, like a natural disaster in my own world. At these times, I become extremely serious about prayer and go to the trenches. I pull out my *Quiet Time Notebook,* and I use many of my prayer growth plan pages. First, I devote one page to all the troubles weighing on my heart (Adore God in Prayer). Then I write one-sentence prayers to the Lord, crying out to Him about each burden (Prayer Journal). Next, I search deep into Scripture for applicable verses, personalizing them in prayer (Scripture Prayers). Then I listen to God from His Word and write down ideas, thoughts, and actions that come to mind (Listening to God). Finally, I wait patiently and record my thanks for His peace and guidance (Thank You, Lord).

I remember the fear I experienced when I discovered a mass in my side. Even before I told my husband, I wrote out my cry to the Lord in my prayer journal. Every verse in Scripture seemed to speak directly to me. I wrote out my prayers and prayed them aloud. And I waited. God answered my prayer by calming my heart as I underwent many tests. God's deliverance continued, giving me peace as I waited for the results. The mass turned out to be a benign condition. I wish I could say that life is always such a smooth ride to heaven. However, Jesus promises that in this world we will have tribulation (John 16:33), and I can say from personal experience that my own life has borne out the truth of His words. But Jesus also promises that we can take courage, for He has overcome the world (John 16:33). No trouble we can ever face is greater than the power of our Lord (Romans 8:37). What a motivation to cry out to Him in trouble!

The story is told of a young woman with small children who was abandoned by her husband at a truck stop. Devastated and brokenhearted, she sobbed uncontrollably, cowering, anxious, and afraid at a corner booth with her children. A sheriff's officer was called to help. When he arrived, he immediately spotted the woman with her two young daughters. When he asked, "What's the problem?" she poured her heart out to him. "We're flat broke. We don't even have enough money to make a phone call. I'm sitting here praying about what to do next. I want to know God is listening."

The officer, who was also a Christian, nodded, praying silently that God would help this woman. He then asked, "Do you have family?"

She said, "The nearest is in Chicago."

As they continued to talk, the waitress brought food and said, "No charge. We know what's going on here."

Then, one of the truckers walked over to the table and held out a fistful of money, "Here...we passed the hat. There ought to be enough to get the woman and her girls started on their way." In just minutes, enough money had been collected to send all three to Chicago.

When the woman saw the money, she began to sob again. She whispered through her tears, "He heard."[3]

And you too can know that even in your most dark and desperate hour, God hears your cries and will deliver you. He promises.

My Response

DATE:

KEY VERSE: "The righteous cry, and the LORD hears and delivers them out of all their troubles" (Psalm 34:17).

FOR FURTHER THOUGHT: How have you seen God answer your prayers and respond to you in a time of trouble? In what ways do you need to cry out to your Lord today?

MY RESPONSE:

Day Twenty

THE GREAT
SURPRISE OF GOD

Call to Me and I will answer you,
and I will tell you great and mighty
things, which you do not know.

JEREMIAH 33:3

Passionate prayer broadens your spiritual vision, opening your eyes, heart, mind, and soul to God's divine activity in your life and to those in the world around you. When you walk and talk with God, you gain spiritual sensitivity, receptivity, and perceptivity. Your spiritual sensitivity toward Him is heightened, your ears are receptive to what He has to say, and your mind, heart, and soul are fully opened to understand what He reveals. Prayer takes you on a journey that others miss because they do not pray. You are led through the myriads of trials and obstacles into the fulfillment of His magnificent plans and purposes.

This principle of spiritual vision is taught throughout the Bible (Proverbs 29:18; 2 Corinthians 4:17-18; 5:7), but it is clearly evidenced in the life of Jeremiah. Jeremiah lived in a turbulent time of godlessness. His own people threatened his life and when Babylon destroyed Jerusalem, Jeremiah lived with exiles in Egypt. God appealed to Jeremiah in the midst of his suffering, "Call to Me and I will answer you, and I will tell you great and mighty things, which you do not know." These words encouraged Jeremiah to engage in an activity that would result in a new vision for life and a new understanding of God and His work in the world. What was that activity that God invited Jeremiah to engage in? Prayer—not just any kind of prayer, but specific and expectant prayer.

I like to think of spiritual vision as the ability to see God's activity in a godless world. The writer of Proverbs says, "Where there is no vision, the people perish" (Proverbs 29:18 KJV). The Hebrew word translated "vision" is *hazon* (a divine communication from God). In the New Testament, the Greek word translated "vision" following the transfiguration event (Matthew 17:9) is *horama* and implies a sight divinely granted. Matthew Henry comments on the Matthew sequence that the vision of the transfiguration for the disciples "was intended to support their faith." We see a cause and effect between prayer and spiritual vision (Psalms 50:15; 91:15). Our action is to call upon the Lord, and God supplies the result—spiritual vision.

Is it possible to live in the industrialized world without a cell phone? It would seem not. The worldwide handset market is nearly two billion units at the time of this writing. Even children have cell phones. Making a phone call to someone wirelessly is an amazing feat to me. I can be stepping out of a restaurant or walking in the mall, and in an instant I'm in touch with a friend, family member, or business. However, there is one important prerequisite. I must know the phone number. Otherwise, all the technology in the world is not going to help me make that call.

Jeremiah 33:3 has been called God's phone number. For He says, "Call to me and I will answer you." The Hebrew word translated "call" is *qara* and denotes a purposeful cry or call to a specific recipient. God promises that when you call Him personally, you can expect Him to answer you personally. His answer depends on your call. What an incredible concept! Just imagine that God, the Creator of the universe, is waiting for you to call Him. And He not only promises to answer but also promises to show you "great and mighty things, which you do not know."

In the case of Jeremiah, who saw nothing but defeat and desolation, he was given a spiritual vision of health, healing, and restoration for the people of Israel. Remarkably, God gave Jeremiah a view of the Messiah, who would come and save His people: "In those days and at that time I will cause a righteous Branch of David to spring forth; and He shall execute justice and righteousness on the earth...the LORD is our righteousness..." (Jeremiah 33:15-16). What a surprising revelation to Jeremiah! And that's what God does. He surprises you just when you least expect it.

Remember that the word of the Lord, God's request for Jeremiah to call on Him, came in one of the darkest times of Jeremiah's life. He was confined in the court of the guard by Zedekiah, king of Judah, while the army of Babylon was besieging Jerusalem. God often gives us the greatest vision in the deepest valleys. Arthur Bennett says in his prayer in *The Valley of Vision*, "Lord, in the daytime stars can be seen from deepest wells, and the deeper the wells the brighter thy stars shine." I love that prayer and pray it often.

Dear friend, do you need a new spiritual view, a new spiritual vision, a new spiritual perspective? Call out to God with an open Bible, for God speaks in His Word. And His Word will come alive. Don't be surprised if words begin leaping off the pages with a deeper meaning than you had ever hoped or imagined. Verses you never noticed before become significant. You can depend on God to give you a great and mighty view of His eternal perspective. All He makes known to you is what He has been waiting to show you. He's been waiting for one thing—your call to Him.

George Mueller learned the importance of calling on God when he studied the life of George Whitefield, a man known to have read the Bible on his knees. Mueller believed the Bible to be God-given liturgy and litany— a divine prayer-book, helping God's people call to Him. A.T. Pierson describes calling to God as a "prayer habit, on the knees, with the Word open," and he says this provides a "sacred channel of approach to God." He continues, "The inspired Scriptures form the vehicle of the Spirit in communicating to us the knowledge of the will of God. If we think of God on the one side and man on the other, the Word of God is the mode of conveyance from God to man, of His own mind and heart."[1]

While calling out to God one day, George Mueller's soul was deeply moved by the phrase "a father of the fatherless" from Psalm 68:5. In that verse God gave to Mueller the care of orphans as a life ministry. Mueller responded, "By the help of God, this shall be my argument before Him, respecting the orphans, in the hour of need. He is their Father, and therefore has pledged Himself, as it were, to provide for them; and I have only to remind Him of the need of these poor children in order to have it supplied." This was spiritual vision from God translated into prayer, life, deeds, and service for Mueller's life.

In 1832 Mueller began an orphanage with only two shillings, but he received more than $7,500,000 from the Lord to his ministry over the next 60 years. And Mueller never told anyone but God about his needs. He started 117 schools and educated more than 120,000 children. He built and bought buildings, paid staff, supported missionaries, and fed hundreds of children. Sometimes he would pray at the dinner table in front of empty plates—only to have the food arrive just in time.

How does such a trusting heart and life of faith with spiritual vision begin to develop? By learning to call to God and depend on His promise to answer and to show you great and mighty things that you do not know. Just imagine how much we will miss if we do not call. I remember returning from a weekend trip many years ago to find a note placed on my pillow: "David Martin called—will call early next week." I still have that note, and it is precious to me, for David Martin became my husband. What if he had not called and I had not called back?

I would venture to say that every important spiritual defining moment in my own life may be traced back to a time when I called out to God. God has always responded in specific and significant ways, such as leading me to change my behavior, revealing His character to me, and guiding me to a new direction in ministry. I wonder what great moves of God and life changing ministries might have been missed had devoted men and women not been faithful to call out to their God. I believe God is looking for people who are not content with the status quo, but who are willing to venture out beyond simple understanding and gain new spiritual vision from God Himself. He is waiting for His people to call to Him. Henry Ford once said, "If I had asked my customers what they wanted, they would have told me 'a faster horse.'" God has said, "For as the heavens are higher than the earth, so are My ways higher than your ways and My thoughts than your thoughts" (Isaiah 55:9).

What is the great secret that will take you beyond the "faster horse" to a great vision? Calling out to God. Let us always call on God with a listening ear and an expectant heart. And may we never cease our calling. I wonder what would happen if we called on God as often as we call on our cell phones? May you and I be those faithful ones to call on God in our generation.

My Response

DATE:

KEY VERSE: "Call to Me and I will answer you, and I will tell you great and mighty things, which you do not know" (Jeremiah 33:3).

FOR FURTHER THOUGHT: Can you think of a time when God answered you in a surprising way, demonstrating His great power in your life? In what way do you need the surprise of a new view, a new perspective, a new vision from God today?

MY RESPONSE:

Day Twenty-One

THE GREAT GOODNESS OF GOD

*If you then, being evil, know how to give
good gifts to your children, how much more
will your Father who is in heaven give
what is good to those who ask Him!*

MATTHEW 7:11

You can always trust in the absolute goodness of God when you pray. God's goodness eliminates any fear or dread in the hearts of His children. You may throw caution to the wind, run boldly into the throne room of your heavenly Father, and present every one of your needs. Jesus, when He gave His Sermon on the Mount, made a point to tell His listeners of the goodness of God, His Father, by saying, "If you then, being evil, know how to give good gifts to your children, how much more will your Father who is in heaven give what is good to those who ask Him!" The Greek word translated "good" is *agathos,* and means upright and honorable, best and benevolent, and emphasizes the great depth of the Father's goodness and generosity. Many publishers title Matthew 7:7-12 as "Prayer and the Golden Rule." Goodness and prayer go hand in hand.

One day, my little niece Kayla ran up to me, grabbed my hand, and said, "Aunt Catherine, I would like a dictionary."

I said, "Really, Kayla? Why?"

She said, "Because I want to learn to write books."

Well, you can imagine how proud I was of my Kayla. I asked, "What kind of dictionary would you like, Kayla?"

"A big one! With all the words in it."

How do you think I responded to her request? Did I want to make her pay for a dictionary? Did I want to withhold from her the very item she desired? No! I wanted to give her what she asked for and more. What do you think I did? I went online and bought her not just one dictionary, but two—a child's dictionary and then a beautiful leather-bound thumb-indexed dictionary. Then I bought her many books to feed her desire to be a writer, including a bookmaking kit for children. Kayla received 15 books from her aunt that birthday. I'll admit I did go overboard, but I love Kayla so much I would do just about anything for her. And so it is with the expression of goodness from our heavenly Father.

God has perfect love and eternal goodness. His gifts are a bounty, waiting to be given out of His heart of overflowing love. Indeed, you and I are encouraged by Jesus to ask God for whatever is on our hearts. Jesus said, "Ask, and it will be given to you; seek, and you will find; knock, and it will be opened to you. For everyone who asks receives, and he who seeks finds, and to him who knocks it will be opened" (Matthew 7:7-8). James gives us even more insight into our asking and receiving from God: "You do not have because you do not ask" (James 4:2). You might think of these words as a promise in reverse, but the intent is that our receiving is often dependent on our willingness to ask. And that willingness is directly related to our ongoing fellowship with the Lord. God is just waiting to pour out His blessings on us. It is not that God is withholding His blessing, but He pours out His blessing to His children who ask in the context of an intimate relationship with their loving Father. Just imagine your God asking you, "Child, what do you want?"

One of my favorite ways to pray is to imagine myself in God's throne room, before my Lord, who is inviting me to pray to Him. This way of praying has become such a frequent habit for me that I like to devote a Prayer Focus page in my notebook. (See figure 11 for an example.) On

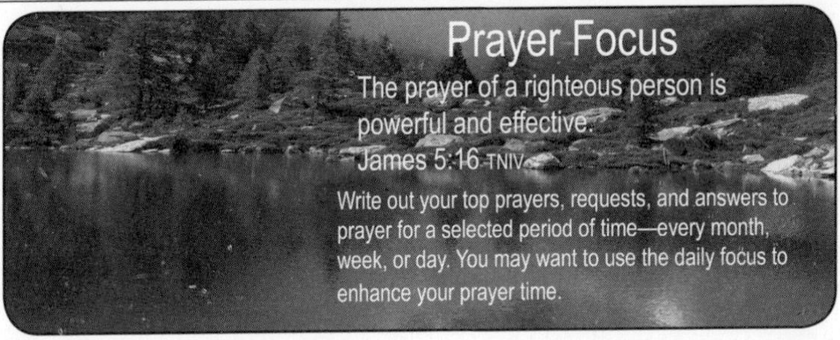

Prayer Focus

The prayer of a righteous person is powerful and effective.
—James 5:16 TNIV

Write out your top prayers, requests, and answers to prayer for a selected period of time—every month, week, or day. You may want to use the daily focus to enhance your prayer time.

My Prayers

Dates—Month, Week, or Day
4-1-07

1. Messages on spiritual growth for upcoming SCC Women's Retreat from 2 Peter 3:18
2. The next books I write—a book on the adventure of knowing God and one on prayer
3. My dear mother
4. My organization of time this next year to accomplish much in Your name, dear Lord.
5. The filming of msg. for Walking with the God who Cares

A—Adoration   C—Confession   T—Thanksgiving   S—Supplication
Daily Focus: Sunday—church, pastors, leaders, Monday—country, Tuesday—the world, Wednesday—community, Thursday—missionaries and ministries, Friday—your ministry, Saturday—revival

God's Answers

1. April 2007 4 messages that led to a new book on spiritual growth
2. July 2008 Lord, thank You for helping me write two books all about trusting in Your names.
3. Dec 2007 Thank You, Lord, for guiding us.
4. 3-2008 Thank You, Lord, for giving me the discipline to do more than I thought I could do.
5. 6-2007 Thank You, Lord, for a great location and Your strength.

What I'm learning:
4-1-08 I am learning to walk and live by faith. I would say my big words over the last year have been trust, faith, and believe.

Enriching Your Life of Prayer © 1998, 2008 Catherine Martin

Figure 11

this page I list my top five prayer requests for special focus. You could also use a blank page in your journal or notebook. I think, *If I could ask God anything, what would I ask?*

Friends, this is a very powerful way to pray, for you will often ask Him for things that may seem bold or even extraordinary. But God delights in just such prayers. You never want it to be said that you don't have because you never asked. You may ask, "Isn't that a kind of selfish or presumptuous praying?" Be encouraged; God already knows what is in your heart. You will discover that God will often lead you to change your prayers to even more extraordinary requests!

I remember hearing Rick Warren share how he prayed for an achievable number of small groups to study *The Purpose-Driven Life.* When he prayed that prayer, he was ultimately led by God to pray for an impossible number of small groups to be formed. God answered above and beyond even that impossible number.

Passionate prayer becomes presumptuous when we begin to demand an answer and demand a specific result. Nowhere in Scripture are we encouraged to tell God what He is going to do. I have heard some say that we need to claim God's Word in such a way that we visualize it until it happens. I cannot even imagine talking in this manner with God. God alone possesses the full knowledge of His plan and purpose, not me. However, God asks us to bring His promises in His Word to Him in our prayers, lay out our heart's desires, and then wait patiently. We must have the heart of David, who said, "In the morning, I will order my prayer to You and eagerly watch" (Psalm 5:3). Oh, may God raise up an army of such eager, praying hearts among the people of God!

God often pours out good gifts in spite of our *not* asking or requesting. James explains, "Every good and perfect gift is from above, coming down from the Father of lights, with whom there is no variation or shifting shadow" (James 1:17). However, His Word does encourage us that He will give abundantly to those who ask extravagantly, knowing the Father has an abundant, overflowing heart (Ephesians 3:20-21). I've prayed some extravagant prayers in my time, and I've seen God more than match a prayer with an extravagant answer. Very early on in Quiet Time Ministries, I remember praying for a CD printer and duplicator, a quite expensive and extravagant item at the time. We received a donation for almost the exact dollar amount on that same day. When I started speaking at retreats and conferences, I prayed for a van for Quiet Time Ministries to carry quiet time materials to area events. Someone presented the keys to a new van that same week. And personally, when I was single, living in remote Julian, California, working for Josh McDowell, I prayed for my future husband on one day in particular—August 11. Soon after we became engaged, I learned from David that he had prayed for his future wife on his birthday. Guess what day that was—that same August 11! God's goodness is written all through the story of my life, and often I see His goodness best when I have prayed the most.

Moses made an extravagant, over-the-top request on Mount Sinai. After a series of prayers requests, Moses finally cried out to God, "Now show me your glory" (Exodus 33:18 NIV). Moses wanted more from God than he had ever received before. And his bold prayer so pleased God that He responded with a hearty yes to Moses' request. The Lord said, "I will cause all my goodness to pass in front of you, and I will proclaim my name, the LORD, in your presence." In this case, the Hebrew word translated "goodness" is *towb* (good, pleasant, beautiful, excellent, lovely). His goodness encompassed many qualities—compassion, grace, slowness to anger, loving-kindness, truth, forgiveness, and justice. As a result, Moses experienced a face-to-face encounter with God that few in history have ever experienced—all because Moses had asked. How could Moses make such a bold request? He counted on the goodness of God.

When it comes to your life of passionate prayer, I consider God's goodness one of the most important promises in the Bible. The sons of Korah asserted in Psalm 84:11, "For the LORD God is a sun and shield; the LORD gives grace and glory; no good thing does He withhold from those who walk uprightly." He is not a withholding God, but a giving God who gives good things. And so, as a child who is going to ask from his or her Father, you must understand the goodness of your God as completely as possible. James Montgomery Boice summarizes the concept:

> If a young man wants to ask his father for something, he will pattern his request on the nature and the temperament of his father. If the father is ill-tempered and stingy, the young man will ask for little. He will take care to present his need in the most winsome and unobjectionable manner. If the father is

good-natured and generous, the child will present his need openly and with great confidence. It is the same spiritually. If a man prays, he will pray in harmony with his view of the God to whom he is praying.[1]

Your understanding of the nature of your God will determine the character of your requests.

Oh, how great and magnificent is the goodness of God! A.W. Tozer points out that "the whole outlook of mankind might be changed if we could all believe that we dwell under a friendly sky and that the God of heaven, though exalted in power and majesty, is eager to be friends with us."[2] The goodness of God is the foundation of our expectation. And our expectation, our hope in our God, will motivate many prayers. Why? Because trusting in His goodness allays many fears and makes us bold in our approach to God.

Hannah Whitall Smith described her discovery of God's goodness in her book *The God of all Comfort*. She was reading Psalm 34:8: "O taste and see that the LORD is good." She had read those words many times, but this time was different:

> Suddenly they meant something. The LORD is good, I repeated to myself. What does it mean to be good? What, but this, the living up to the best and highest that one knows. To be good is exactly opposite of being bad. To be bad is to know the right and not to do it, but to be good is to do the best we know. And I saw that, since God is omniscient, He must know what is the best and highest good of all, and that, therefore His goodness must necessarily be beyond question.[3]

Hannah Whitall Smith discovered in the goodness of God that "nothing could possibly go wrong under His care." She wondered how she could ever possibly be anxious again when realizing the true goodness of God.

And yet we do, at times, question God's goodness when circumstances don't turn out the way we had hoped or imagined. When I am frustrated by a turn of events, I often turn my thoughts to the goodness of God and remind myself with a smile, *There must be something in God's mind that has not yet entered my own thoughts.* I have learned this practice from the words of God in Isaiah 55:9, where He tells me His ways are higher than my ways. God may not always give us what we want or package His blessings in the wrapping we desire, but He does always give what is best and according to His goodness.

The divine answer for our questions into the mysteries of God is to "taste and see that the LORD is good." We must *press through* and pray to God, walking and talking with Him moment by moment. This pressing through is at the heart of passionate prayer. George Mueller wrestled in prayer when his daughter became deathly ill with typhoid fever.

> Of all the trials of faith that as yet I have had to pass through, this was the greatest; and by God's abundant mercy, I own it to His praise, I was enabled to delight myself in the will of God; for I felt perfectly sure, that, if the Lord took this beloved daughter, it would be best for her parents, best for herself, and more for the glory of God than if she lived: this better part I was satisfied with; and thus my heart had peace, perfect peace, and I had not a moment's anxiety.[4]

George Mueller's statement may on the surface seem too harsh to handle. Yet we must consider his conclusion, for is it not true that life is not always easy, and circumstances often seem impossible? Even Jesus prayed such a prayer in the garden of Gethsemane, knowing that the cross lay ahead. He prayed, "Father, if You are willing, remove this cup from Me; yet not My will, but Yours be done" (Luke 22:42). When we pray, we must press through to the heart of God—who He is, what He does, and what He says. When we do, we will gain a new vision of God's goodness.

God sometimes seems to be silent. Our trials sometimes seem to drag on and on. Sometimes we cannot interpret the pattern of God in our lives. Those are the days when we must count on God's goodness by faith. And pray—passionately and wholeheartedly. When we press through to God in prayer, calculating His goodness into our circumstances, our faith will grow stronger, and our relationship with God will grow deeper. We will discover, on the other side of those trials, that we are seemingly ten thousand steps closer to God.

When Mueller's beloved wife died, God empowered him to say, "The Lord was good and did good: first, in giving her to me; second, in so long leaving her to me; and third, in taking her from me."[5] He chose as his text for the funeral, Psalm 119:68; "You are good and do good." You may not be dealing with the death of a loved one, but with the death of a dream. What you were wishing to happen for your life has fallen short of your desire. Sometimes God says no to one thing in order to say yes to the best thing. The best may require a wait for the perfect timing of God. But you can always count on this truth—God is good all the time. He is not the author of evil (James 1:13). And so we must press through to see, understand, and experience His goodness anew. We would be encouraged to heartily join the chorus of the psalmist and sing, "O taste and see that the LORD is good." And then we will pray.

DATE:

KEY VERSE: "If you then, being evil, know how to give good gifts to your children, how much more will your Father who is in heaven give what is good to those who ask Him!" (Matthew 7:11).

FOR FURTHER THOUGHT: What impresses you the most about God's goodness? In what area of your life do you need to understand and apply God's goodness? How does knowing and understanding the goodness of God motivate you to pray?

MY RESPONSE:

Day Twenty-Two

THE GREAT HELP
OF GOD

*In the same way the Spirit also helps our
weakness; for we do not know how to pray as
we should, but the Spirit Himself intercedes
for us with groanings too deep for words.*

ROMANS 8:26

God Himself is the helper for your life of passionate prayer. If you don't know what to pray, God will help you. Even if you don't have the heart to pray, especially then, God will help you. How does He help? You have this promise in His Word: "In the same way the Spirit also helps our weakness; for we do not know how to pray as we should, but the Spirit Himself intercedes for us with groanings too deep for words." We learn from this single verse that God is our provider and our helper.

Jesus promised in John 14:16, "I will ask the Father, and He will give you another Helper, that He may be with you forever; that is the Spirit of truth." As our Helper with a capital *H,* the Holy Spirit knows exactly what we need and how to help us. The Greek word translated "Helper" is *parakletos* and refers to one who pleads another's cause and one who is called

175

alongside to help. In Romans 8:26-27, we see four essential benefits of the Holy Spirit in our life of prayer:

1. He helps our weaknesses.
2. He gives us access to the Father.
3. He intercedes for us.
4. He knows, desires, and prays God's will for us.

Let's examine these helps.

What a benefit to have one in our lives who not only sees our weaknesses but also comes alongside to help, often at the very point of our failure. The Holy Spirit's nature is to help. Our primary weakness in prayer is not knowing how or what to pray. When it comes to prayer, man is poised to fail if left only to his own devices. The power of prayer is greater than any man can grasp. But the Holy Spirit never leaves us to ourselves, never abandons us, and always stays with us to help.

One of the gifts given by God through the Holy Spirit is the Word of God itself (2 Peter 1:21). When we open the Bible, the Holy Spirit makes the words come alive. The Holy Spirit precisely selects, with perfect timing, the verses we need to hear for the circumstances we face. Only God truly sees our life experience for what it really is. Only God knows what we need. The Holy Spirit not only helps us by teaching us from God's Word but also gives us spiritual discernment. Paul tells us in 1 Corinthians 2:12-16 that through the Holy Spirit we have "the mind of Christ," we may "know the things freely given to us by God," and we can "appraise" or discern all things. Remember our Oswald Chambers quote from *My Utmost for His Highest:* "Discernment is God's call to intercession, never to faultfinding."[1] I've never forgotten these words. When God gives me a window into a particular circumstance, He encourages me to take what I see to Him in prayer. I always look at discernment as God's help in my weakness.

Another benefit of the Holy Spirit in prayer is that He takes us directly to the Father. In Ephesians 2:18 we see that "through Him [Jesus] we both have our access in one Spirit to the Father." Paul tells us in Romans 8:16 that "the Spirit Himself testifies with our spirit that we are children of God." As God's children, we are given the privilege to cry out "Abba! Father!" and experience the intimacy of a child who says, "Daddy" or "Papa." We are told in Hebrews 4:16 to "draw near with confidence to the throne of grace, so that we may receive mercy and find grace to help in time of need." But how can we truly experience access into the heavenly throne room and draw near? The indwelling Holy Spirit personally takes us into the throne room, assures us of our relationship with God, and gives us the boldness and courage to cry out to the Father.

Larry Crabb, in his book *The Papa Prayer,* pictures our access to our Abba, Father this way. He likens us to the young children of the president of the United States, with complete access to the Oval Office. We are "able to climb up in our Papa's lap while He commands armies across the world in the real war against terror. As we listen from our cozy vantage point, we begin to understand what our heavenly Papa is up to."[2] God desires our presence more than any other thing. He desires an intimate relationship of communion and conversation. The Holy Spirit draws us to the heart of the Father. And that is where we need to be if we desire to walk and talk with God.

Yet another benefit is that the Holy Spirit intercedes for us. In the Holy Spirit's intercession, we see Him doing for us what we cannot do for ourselves. Even when we are not praying, He is praying for us. What an encouragement this is to me at all times. Sometimes I'm too tired to pray. Sometimes I'm so brokenhearted and crushed in spirit, I don't have any strength to pray. Sometimes I just don't know what to pray. And yet the Holy Spirit prays in a way that is deeper than words, and God the Father always hears His prayers.

No prayers are more passionate than the prayers of God. And nowhere is this more evident than in the Holy Spirit's intercession for us with "groanings too deep for words." C.E.B. Cranfield says in his Romans commentary, "The Spirit's groanings are not spoken, because they do not need to be, since God knows the Spirit's intention without its being expressed."[3] Such sighs that go deeper than words indicate He labors intensely for us. As William Newell says in his book *Romans Verse by Verse,* "The Spirit, who knows the vast abysmal need of every one of us, knows that need to the least possible particular. 'Groanings which cannot be uttered' expresses at once the vastness of our need, our utter ignorance and inability, and the infinite concern of the blessed indwelling Spirit for us."[4] Dear friend, don't you at times sense a certain groaning in your own heart that never completely surfaces to words? According to this verse, we are completely unaware of the depth of the passion of the Holy Spirit on our behalf. And therein lies a multiplication of our encouragement.

One other benefit is that the Holy Spirit knows, desires, and prays God's will for us. Here we see that God works on our behalf regardless of how weak or foolish we may be. The Spirit knows God's heart for us and prays in exact harmony with His desires. How does He help our prayers? He will change your prayers. The work of the Holy Spirit includes leading, guiding, and directing. His prayers lead your prayers according to the will of God (Romans 8:27). Guess what verse follows next? Romans 8:28. "And we know that God causes all things to work together for good to those who love God, to those who are called according to His purpose." Isn't it fitting that this oft-quoted verse follows the truth of the Spirit's prayers for us?

During his chaplaincy of the United States Senate, Dr. Richard Halverson became increasingly aware of one basic fact: "The deepest problems of this world are mostly beyond man's ability to find a solution."[5] He describes the myriad difficulties he observed from his unique vantage point in Washington DC, recounting the statistics of teenage suicide, drug addiction, and prostitution, and he concludes, "I feel deeply about these problems. I also feel frustration and futility. There's nothing I can do, except pray, and often I don't know how to pray. It is then I remember those verses in Romans."[6] Halverson gave his body to be "a groaning ground for God." God used Dr. Halverson's helplessness to accomplish the highest and greatest purposes. May we do the same. May we all become a groaning ground for God.

My Response

DATE:

KEY VERSE: "In the same way the Spirit also helps our weakness; for we do not know how to pray as we should, but the Spirit Himself intercedes for us with groanings too deep for words" (Romans 8:26).

FOR FURTHER THOUGHT: Describe what you have learned about the Holy Spirit's help in your prayers. Why do we need His help? How do you need His help today in your own life?

MY RESPONSE:

THE GREAT PEACE
OF GOD

*Be anxious for nothing, but in everything by prayer
and supplication with thanksgiving, let your
requests be made known to God. And the peace
of God, which surpasses all comprehension, will
guard your hearts and your minds in Christ Jesus.*

PHILIPPIANS 4:6-7

Prayer is God's prescription for a troubled heart. The more you pray, the more you experience God's peace. Peace is passionate prayer's great result. Paul encouraged the suffering church of Philippi, "Be anxious for nothing, but in everything by prayer and supplication with thanksgiving let your requests be made known to God. And the peace of God, which surpasses all comprehension, will guard your hearts and your minds in Christ Jesus." If you are worried or anxious, you must pray. If you are angry, you must pray. If you are bitter, you must pray. If you are fearful, you must pray. The heart's deepest troubles require your most passionate prayers. God's peace will stand as a guard over the heart, patrolling every door of entry and blocking out all worry, anxiety, anger, and fear.

Renée Bondi was 29 and engaged to be married when she experienced a bizarre accident that left her a quadriplegic. She married her beloved Mike and, miraculously, became pregnant. About a week before her delivery date, she received some news that sent her into an emotional tailspin and into a dark night of the soul: Her sister, Michelle, had also suffered an accident and was left paralyzed—a paraplegic. Renée fell into an acute state of anger and bitterness. She cried out to God, "Why did You let this happen? Isn't one member of our family enough! You could have stopped the accident. You could have protected her from a broken back. Why didn't You! Don't You care? Where are You?"[1]

Renée became angry with God and everyone else. For two months her anger ruled her life and engulfed her heart. Suddenly one day, during an angry exchange with her husband, she stopped in mid-sentence, looking at the distressed face of her beloved. Her heart was pierced, and she knew what she must do. "God, I surrender this anger. I ask You to replace my anger with Your peace. I knew it at one time. I don't know it now…Lord, I give up my right to be angry. I surrender it to You. Take it from me and replace it with Your peace."[2] With each new prayer, a new calm entered her heart.

About two months later, while at lunch with a friend, Renée found herself laughing at something her friend said. Then she realized, "You did it, Lord! You really did replace my anger with Your peace." Renée's defining moment came when she surrendered the troubles of her heart to the one she calls the King of Peace, and she invited Him to guard her heart with His peace.

Oh, what a defining moment we may experience when we take all fear, worry, bitterness, and anger, and lay it all at the feet of *Yahweh Shalom* (The Lord Is Peace). The New Testament word translated "peace" is *eirene* and refers to tranquility based on a sense of divine favor. When storms rage in your heart, follow the example of the disciples who were with their Lord on the stormy Sea of Galilee. Fearing for their lives, thinking their boat would sink, they cried out to Jesus. "He said to them, 'Why are you afraid, you men of little faith?' Then He got up and rebuked the winds and the sea, and it became perfectly calm" (Matthew 8:25). Imagine the Lord bringing that same calmness to your heart and commanding the tempest in your soul to be still. The peace of God leads to the greatest satisfaction and contentment one can have in life. God's peace brings rest, tranquility, and a sense of safety to the heart.

And so, what must we do when worry, fear, bitterness, or anger come knocking on the door of our hearts and minds? We must pray. The context of the fourth chapter of Philippians is important in understanding how we must pray. Paul has just informed the church that "the Lord is near" (Philippians 4:5). This may be interpreted as realized and future eschatology: The Lord is ever present and coming again.[3] Walking and talking with the Lord depends on His presence in your life. And, as Francis Schaeffer titled his book, *He Is There and He Is Not Silent.* In the magnificent context of God's forever presence with us and in us, He invites us to tell Him "every detail of our needs in earnest and thankful prayer" (Philippians 4:6 Phillips).

God's presence brings a question to our minds. Why would we need to tell God the details of our lives when He already knows what we need? Telling Him draws us into the heavenly courts of the Lord Himself as we spread our cares before Him, lifting us above the temporal and inviting us to breathe in the air of an eternal perspective. Hezekiah learned to present his troubles to the Lord by spreading out an intimidating letter from the king of the Assyrians (2 Kings 19:14; Isaiah 37:14-15). Threatened with destruction of Jerusalem, Hezekiah had to choose to believe the gods of his enemy or to live in the presence of the one true God. We make a similar decision. Our outlook can move from despair to hope and from dread to expectation. R. Rainy explains the impact of prayer in our lives: "The way to be anxious about nothing is to be prayerful about everything."[4]

When God invites you to pray about everything, He is implying that no need is too small to take to Him. I learned this lesson from the Lord in a profound way when my husband and I were in Newport Beach, California, for a medical conference. Just before the conference was to begin, we could not find one of my husband's contact lenses. We searched everywhere. Finally, I decided to get in my car, drive two hours back home, and retrieve his spare pair of lenses.

When I arrived at home, retrieved his spare lenses, and got back in the car to drive yet another two hours back to Newport Beach, a little revival song came to my mind: "What a Friend We Have in Jesus." I began singing, and halfway through the first stanza, tears came to my eyes. "O what peace we often forfeit / O what needless pain we bear / All because we do not carry / Everything to God in prayer." I immediately said, *Lord, I never prayed.* And it was true. I had not asked God about my husband's contact lens. And so, I immediately asked, "Lord, where is that contact lens?" Almost immediately I remembered one place by the bathtub. I had forgotten to look there.

As soon as I arrived at our hotel, I ran to our room and looked on the floor by the tub, and there was my husband's contact lens! I started laughing, realizing that God's promise in Psalm 37:23 is indeed true: "The LORD directs the steps of the godly. He delights in every detail of their lives" (NLT). God is not only the God of the impossible but also the God of details, even the small things.

Paul encourages us to add thanksgiving to our conversation with God. The Greek word translated "thanksgiving" is *eucharistia* and in this context refers to gratitude to God. The word *Eucharist* is used in our language for Communion, our celebration of thanksgiving for the sacrifice of Christ. Paul is encouraging the Philippian church to be thankful in everything. How can we be thankful to God when our hearts are not in the mood? When your heart is broken and crushed, just about the last expression you feel is gratitude. I firmly believe our thankfulness to God, especially in difficult times, is a "by faith" prayer based on who God is, what He does, and what He says in His Word. Thankfulness acknowledges truths beyond that which I know and feel. My gratitude acknowledges God's behind-the-scenes work in the world and in my life. Sometimes what He is doing is eminently visible, but other times it is not apparent. But what if He is doing the most marvelous and amazing work, invisible to our eyes? Often, that is exactly the case. And so let us say, *Thank You, Lord. You are awesome and incredible.* Let us not be unaware, like Jacob, who finally said, "Surely the LORD is in this place, and I did not know it" (Genesis 28:16).

Always remember, dear friend, God is never worried, anxious, or fearful. He knows what you need even before you ask Him (Matthew 6:8), and He promises to supply all your needs (Philippians 4:19). Why do we ever worry? Why do we become anxious? These questions seem absurd to us because we could probably list at least a thousand reasons why. But Jesus must wonder why His children are constantly worried and prone to anxiety, when He knows the provision of the Father for our needs. He encourages us not to worry about what we will eat, what we will wear, where we will live, or even the pressure and passage of time (Matthew 6:25-34). Jesus says, "Your heavenly Father knows that you need all these things" (Matthew 6:32), implying He will provide for our basic needs in life.

When Renée Bondi shares her testimony, she sings the song "Be Not Afraid." This song is taken from Deuteronomy 20:1, where the people of Israel were encouraged not to be afraid, for the LORD their God was with them. "Be Not Afraid" is a reminder of the peace and presence of God in Renée's life. Always remember, dear friend, because of God's presence with us and His peace in our hearts, we never need fear or worry. The great peace of God is our sufficiency.

Be Not Afraid

You shall walk the barren desert,
But you shall not die of thirst.
You shall wander far in safety
Though you do not know the way.

You shall speak your words in foreign lands,
And all will understand.
You shall see the face of God and live.

If you pass through raging waters
In the sea, you shall not drown.
If you walk amid the burning flames,
You shall not be harmed.

If you stand before the pow'r of hell
And death is at your side,
Know that I am with you through it all.

Blessed are your poor,
For the kingdom shall be theirs.
Blest are you that weep and mourn,
for one day you shall laugh.

And if wicked tongues insult and hate you
All because of Me,
Blessed, blessed are you!

Be not afraid.
I go before you always.
Come follow Me,
and I will give you rest.[5]

BOB DUFFORD

DATE:

KEY VERSE: "Be anxious for nothing, but in everything by prayer and supplication with thanksgiving let your requests be made known to God. And the peace of God, which surpasses all comprehension, will guard your hearts and your minds in Christ Jesus" (Philippians 4:6-7).

FOR FURTHER THOUGHT: What encouraged you the most today as you considered praying about every detail of your life? How do you need God's peace, and what do you need to take to Him and lay at His feet? Close by writing a prayer to your Lord, expressing all that is on your heart.

MY RESPONSE:

Day Twenty-Four

QUIET TIME
WEEK FOUR:
THE PARTICULARS
OF PRAYER

*In the morning, O LORD, You will hear
my voice; in the morning I will order
my prayer to You and eagerly watch.*

PSALM 5:3

PREPARE YOUR HEART

Learning to pray is a lifelong adventure. And what an adventure! Our approach to God and our conversation and communion with Him are new each day. Just as life is never the same, so our walk and our talk will be filled with fresh subjects and words. But God is the same. And the Bible is filled with instruction for our prayer to Him. Today the goal of your quiet time is to learn different aspects of your conversation with God. Draw near to God now and ask Him to teach you to pray.

READ AND STUDY GOD'S WORD

1. The Bible assumes that you pray. In fact, Paul exhorts us to "pray all the time" (1 Thessalonians 5:17 MSG). How then shall we pray? Today you

are going to look at a number of examples of prayer and ways to pray. Look at the following verses and write out what you learn about prayer. Be sure to personalize what you learn.

2 Samuel 22:4

1 Chronicles 16:9

1 Chronicles 29:13-14

Psalm 5:3

Psalm 18:1

Psalm 40:1

Hosea 6:1-3

Ephesians 6:18

Philippians 4:6-7

1 Timothy 2:1-4

James 5:16

1 John 1:9

2. Look at the following words on prayer from Jesus, and underline those phrases about prayer that mean the most to you today.

"Pray for those who persecute you" (Matthew 5:44).

"When you pray, go into your inner room, close your door and pray to your Father who is in secret, and your Father who sees what is done in secret will reward you" (Matthew 6:6).

"But this kind does not go out except by prayer and fasting" (Matthew 17:21, see Mark 9:29).

"Keep watching and praying that you may not enter into temptation; the spirit is willing, but the flesh is weak" (Matthew 26:41).

"All things for which you pray and ask, believe that you have received them, and they will be granted you" (Mark 11:24).

"Whenever you stand praying, forgive, if you have anything against anyone, so that your Father who is in heaven will also forgive you your transgressions" (Mark 11:25).

"Ask, and it will be given to you; seek, and you will find; knock, and it will be opened to you" (Luke 11:9).

"If you then, being evil, know how to give good gifts to your children, how much more will your heavenly Father give the Holy Spirit to those who ask Him?" (Luke 11:13).

"Now He was telling them a parable to show that at all times they ought to pray and not lose heart" (Luke 18:1).

"But keep on the alert at all times, praying that you may have strength to escape all these things that are about to take place, and to stand before the Son of Man" (Luke 21:36).

3. What is the most important truth you have learned about prayer today that you can apply to your own life?

ADORE GOD IN PRAYER

David is a great example of one who prayed. He said, "In the morning, O LORD, You will hear my voice; In the morning I will order my prayer to You and eagerly watch." He learned to "order" his prayer. He laid his prayer out to the Lord and fashioned it in words as he conversed with God. From your study today, you learned that there is much to pray about and many ways to pray, including praise, worship, petition, thanksgiving, and confession. The acrostic ACTS is a good way to remember the ways to pray. Draw near to God in...

Adoration. Worship God for who He is, what He does, and what He says.

Confession. Ask God to show you any sin in your life then confess your sin to Him.

Thanksgiving. Express gratitude to God for all you can today.

Supplication. Pray for others and yourself.

YIELD YOURSELF TO GOD

How do we pray? In as many different ways as there are people. Some of us pray with our eyes closed; others with our eyes open. Some raise their hands; others lower their heads. Some stand; others kneel. Some pray regularly; others sporadically. Some pray formally; others spontaneously. Some pray throughout the day; others "bookend" their day with morning and evening prayers. Some pray out loud; others in silence. Some pray easily; for others, it takes great effort. We pray in our favorite chair with a hot cup of coffee and a quilt thrown over our legs. We pray kneeling on the hardwood floor by the bassinet of a sick baby. We pray standing in a phone booth. Sitting on a park bench. Lying in a hospital bed. Daniel prayed three times a day at a set time and in a set place. David seems to have been more spontaneous. Moses made lengthy intercession for the Israelites. The publican in the Temple courtyard made a short plea for only himself. Job called out to God in his anger and despair. Mary called out to him in joy and exultation...However they came with their prayers, they came. In their own way. With their own words. Standing or kneeling, they came. Raising their hands or clenching their fists, they came. Full of food or fasting, they came. And maybe there's something to be learned from that. Maybe it's not so important how we come...but that we come.[1]

KEN GIRE

ENJOY HIS PRESENCE

Imagine that you have been given an audience with God Himself and can talk with Him about anything you'd like. What would you say? Would you ask Him for something? Would you say "I'm sorry"? Would you say, "I love You, Lord"? He is waiting even now to talk with you, so turn the eyes of your heart to Him and draw near. May you have a blessed time together with Him.

REST IN HIS LOVE

"First, I tell you to pray for all people, asking God for what they need and being thankful to him. Pray for rulers and for all who have authority so that we can have quiet and peaceful lives full of worship and respect for God. This is good, and it pleases God our Savior, who wants all people to be saved and know the truth" (1 Timothy 2:1-4 NCV).

Notes—Week Four

PASSION FOR YOUR LIFE OF PRAYER

Days 25–30

Day Twenty-Five

WARFARE PRAYER

*Put on the full armor of God so that you can
fight against the devil's evil tricks. Our fight
is not against people on earth but against
the rulers and authorities and the power of
this world's darkness, against the spiritual
powers of evil in the heavenly world.*

EPHESIANS 6:11-12 NCV

In our journey into a life of passionate prayer, we must become prayer warriors. Learning and practicing the art of warfare prayer is an imperative for every disciple of Christ. We are in a spiritual war, as Paul explains: "Our fight is not against people on earth but against the rulers and authorities and the power of this world's darkness, against the spiritual powers of evil in the heavenly world." And according to Paul, we must effectively deploy prayer as one of our offensive weapons in spiritual battle.

We cannot limit prayer to times of walking and talking in the quiet peace of the garden. Warfare prayer becomes an intense labor of sober, earnest pleading and anguish. Paul continues, "With all prayer and petition pray at all times in the Spirit, and with this in view, be on the alert with all perseverance and petition for all the saints" (Ephesians 6:18). For when we battle in prayer, we see spiritual "strongholds" destroyed (2 Corinthians 10:4 NIV), or "the destruction of fortresses" (NASB). Paul encourages us with a reminder that we are emboldened by divine power when we wield the weapons of our warfare. He goes on to explain that these weapons destroy "speculations and every lofty thing raised up against the knowledge of God."

Elizabeth Alves, in her book *Becoming a Prayer Warrior,* tells the story of an evangelist in Latin America who was witnessing and passing out tracts to people on the streets. In one city, he met great opposition on one side of the provincial boundary that divided the area. The people literally threw the gospel tracts on the ground and refused to listen to him. When the evangelist crossed the street into the other province, he was stunned at the welcome reception to the gospel, everyone eager to receive the tracts about Jesus. The evangelist wondered, *Why is there such a difference?* Sometime later he discovered that a group of Christians in the second province had been praying for the gospel to be preached, taking up the full armor of God in spiritual battle to bind the forces of darkness.

How can we become effective, even great prayer warriors? We first must make certain we are spiritually armed, be aware of our opposition (hindrances to prayer), and use our spiritual weapons effectively (Ephesians 6:10-18). The more we pray, the more we grow in our relationship with Christ. And the more we are used by the Lord in His plans and purposes, the more likely we are to be targeted by the enemy as a threat. We must learn what protects us spiritually and take great care that our armor has no chinks or weaknesses. Paul says, "Therefore, take up the full armor of God, so that you will be able to resist in the evil day, and having done everything, to stand firm" (Ephesians 6:13). The Greek word translated "full armor" is *panoplia* and refers to the heavy equipment used by the Greek army. The English word *panoply* emphasizes the whole, as in "nothing less than the whole (the full armor) will do." In fierce battle, those who become complacent and undisciplined begin to lay aside some of their armor, become weak spiritually, and thus render themselves as open targets to the enemy. And so we must periodically take spiritual inventory as an act of faith, praying through all areas of our spiritual life, viewing them as the constitution of our spiritual armor.

The first piece of armor is the belt of truth. It prepares you for any battle that may come your way and holds the other pieces of armor in place. Pray, *Lord, You are the truth. Fill my mind with the truth of Your Word. Help me know the truth so well that I can easily recognize anything that is a lie, and help me speak the truth.*

The breastplate of righteousness is the life of sanctification or holiness produced by the Holy Spirit, and it guards your heart. One writer of the book of Proverbs says, "Guard your heart above all else, for it determines the course of your life" (Proverbs 4:23 NLT). Pray, *Lord, You are my righteousness. Live Your life in and through me, help me to be sensitive to the Holy Spirit, show me my sin, grow in me the fruit of the Holy Spirit, and purify my heart, that I might glorify You.*

Your shoes are the gospel, the good news of Jesus Christ. Wherever you go, always be ready to tell others about Christ, living your life in such a way that others will ask about the hope you have. Pray, *Lord, You are the good news for all people. Live in and through me and manifest a sweet aroma of the knowledge of You in every place. Give me boldness and courage and love to share You with a lost and hurting world.*

Your shield is faith, protecting all your other armor and enabling you to stand firm. We are to walk by faith, not by sight (2 Corinthians 5:7), and the victory that overcomes the world is faith (1 John 5:4). Without faith we cannot please God (Hebrews 11:6). Pray, *Lord, I choose to stand on Your Word today. Nothing I face, feel, or see is going to cause me to believe any less than what You say here in the Bible. Help me to walk by faith and not by sight. Give me a life of faith that pleases You.*

Finally, our helmet is salvation, which protects our minds and keeps us from being deceived by the enemy. Pray, *Lord, watch over my mind and save me from any thoughts that could lead me astray. Help me focus on what is true, noble, right, pure, lovely, admirable, excellent, and praiseworthy. Give me a discerning eye and help me always have hope in every circumstance.*

Eugene Peterson paraphrases Ephesians 6:14-17 in a way that helps us understand the practical application of our spiritual armor to our lives. "Truth, righteousness, peace, faith, and salvation are more than words. Learn how to apply them. You'll need them throughout your life." And how true it is. Notice that these five pieces of armor are defensive. J. Vernon McGee points out that these pieces of armor are for the front of a person. He says,

"There is no protection for his back; nothing is provided for retreat. Believe me, a retreating Christian is certainly open season for the enemy."[1] God expects us to stand firm. We must never let down our defenses. We are to be "steadfast, immovable, always abounding in the work of the Lord" knowing that our toil for the Lord is not in vain (1 Corinthians 15:58).

To become prayer warriors, we must also learn to deploy our three offensive spiritual weapons mentioned in Ephesians 6: the Holy Spirit, the Word of God, and prayer. First, we must learn to be filled with the Holy Spirit. The Holy Spirit is mentioned twice in this passage. The Spirit is related to both the Word of God and prayer, and He is essential to their success. Paul says, "Don't be drunk with wine, because that will ruin your life. Instead, be filled with the Holy Spirit" (Ephesians 5:18 NLT).[2] To be filled with the Spirit means you are controlled and empowered by God through the Holy Spirit. What will it take for you to experience His control and power? Surrender control of your life to Him. Confess any sins He brings to your mind. Pray, *Lord fill me with Your Holy Spirit. Control me, empower me, and use me in Your work in the world.*

Next, take up the sword of the Spirit, which is the Word of God. You can never know too much of the Bible. Knowing and loving the Bible is where the heat of the battle has become so fierce in the church today. Fewer and fewer in the church are standing on what God says in His Word. Why? Because many have stopped opening their Bibles on a daily basis. If you don't have the Bible in your heart and mind, you are going to lose the fight. We are to "fight the good fight of faith" according to Paul (1 Timothy 6:12). Oswald Chambers instructs us that the process of making God's Word a personal possession and living it out in our lives is "a fight always, not sometimes."[3] Follow the example of Jesus by answering the lies of the enemy with God's Word: "You say this, but God's Word says…" The great key to taking up the sword of the Spirit is acquiring a personal knowledge of what the Bible says. Jesus encourages us to live our lives like "a wise man who built his house on the rock" (Matthew 7:24). Pray, *Lord, today I stand on Your Word. Help me, day by day, to open the pages of the Bible and live there. Build my life on the truths of what You say in the Bible, and give me strength to live and walk by faith.*

Finally, we must use our offensive weapon of prayer. Oh, how the enemy trembles when you pray. Indeed, the enemy tries to keep you from prayer. Prayer will keep you from the enemy, or the enemy will keep you from prayer. Oswald Chambers exhorts us that prayer is the battle—the "duty is to pray."[4] We must all be soldiers who march to battle on our knees. Always remember that He who is in you is greater than he who is in the world (1 John 4:4). Pray, *Lord, teach me to pray at all times in the Spirit for myself and others, including all the saints. Help me to turn to You in prayer every day to know You, to love You, and to be Your instrument for Your plans and purposes in the world.*

Just as we have three offensive weapons, so we face three constant enemies: the world, the flesh, and the devil. John encourages us never to love the world. He says "all that is in the world, the lust of the flesh and the lust of the eyes and the boastful pride of life, is not from the Father, but is from the world" (1 John 2:16). Jesus tells us that the devil is "a liar and the father of lies" (John 8:44). The enemy will throw his fiery darts at the most inopportune times, especially when you are fatigued (see Luke 4:1-13). Be aware of the hindrances to prayer such as busyness (Mark 6:31), sin (Psalm 66:18), living in the flesh instead of the Spirit (Galatians 5:19-25), doubting (James 1:6), and wrong motives (James 4:3). Charles Spurgeon reminds us that in prayer, as in life itself, "Although we are closely beset and often in sore conflict, we have an Almighty Helper, even Jesus, the Captain of our salvation, who is ever with us, and who assures us that we shall eventually come off more than conquerors through him."[5]

Prayer is a joyful communion with the Creator of the universe. But when we enter the throne room of God, we are also entering the war room of the Commander in Chief. We must remember the magnificent nature of our Commander as seen in the words of David:

> Yours, O LORD, is the greatness and the power and the glory and the victory and the majesty, indeed everything that is in the heavens and the earth; Yours is the dominion, O LORD, and You exalt Yourself as head over all. Both riches and honor come from You, and You rule over all, and in Your hand is power and might; and it lies in Your hand to make great and to strengthen everyone. Now therefore, our God, we thank You, and praise Your glorious name (1 Chronicles 29:11-13).

When God's power is unleashed, there is no battle, for the victory has already been won. Always remember that Jesus is victor. God has given us the victory in Christ (1 Corinthians 15:5). "But in all these things we overwhelmingly conquer through Him who loved us" (Romans 8:37). And so, dear friend, put on your whole armor, take up your spiritual weapons, and engage in the battle with the full knowledge that the Lord is with you as a strong warrior (Jeremiah 20:11). He always wins.

DATE:

KEY VERSE: "Put on the full armor of God so that you can fight against the devil's evil tricks. Our fight is not against people on earth but against the rulers and authorities and the powers of this world's darkness, against the spiritual powers of evil in the heavenly world" (Ephesians 6:11-12 NCV).

FOR FURTHER THOUGHT: What is the most important truth you have learned about warfare prayer, spiritual armor, and your offensive weapons? How does what you have learned help you with what you are experiencing in your life right now?

MY RESPONSE:

INTERCESSORY PRAYER

Pray for one another.
JAMES 5:16

One of our greatest privileges in passionate prayer is to intercede on behalf of others. James encourages each one of us to "pray for one another." This kind of prayer is referred to as "intercessory prayer," implying our commitment to go to God on behalf of others. The Greek word translated "intercession" in Hebrews 7:25 (referring to Christ's intercession for us) is *entugchano* and implies an active process of conversation, consultation, or supplication.

Why pray for others? First, we pray for others because God commands us, as we have seen in James 5:16. We also pray for others because then God's power is unleashed on their behalf. God hears and He responds. Finally, we pray for others out of love for God and love for them. And from the reverse perspective, one of the greatest blessings you will ever receive is when someone walks up to you and says, "I prayed for you." Dear friends, when you see the great needs of others, whether they are family, friends, or strangers, you should not sense overwhelming helplessness. Though you cannot meet their needs yourself, your prayers can make a difference. God is all-sufficient to supply the deepest needs and come to our aid in impossible circumstances.

I was sitting in a planning meeting with about 20 other men and women from our church. My cell phone rang, and I could see from the incoming phone number that the call was from my mother's assisted living home. I stepped out of the room and took the call. The woman on the phone said, "Catherine, we've called the ambulance to take your mother to the hospital. She is suffering some severe side effects from a medication and needs to be evaluated." I gave her the information she needed and then hung up the phone. Of course, I was upset. And yet there was nothing more I could do. My brother was taking care of the situation with my mother. I returned to the meeting and sat down, still reeling from the shock of that phone call.

One of my coworkers at the meeting made a joke about my phone always ringing. I looked into his face and just wanted to cry. He had no idea of the nightmare I was experiencing.

When the meeting ended, I was able to share with a few people what had happened. But really, no one knew or understood. I walked outside to go to my car and drive back to work. As the door closed behind me, it opened again, and another coworker said, "Catherine, wait." I turned around. She said, "Catherine, can I pray for you right now?" She didn't even wait for my response. She put her arm around me and prayed one of the most beautiful prayers I've ever heard. I began sobbing, and she just continued praying. An indescribable peace came over me. When she was finished praying, she looked into my eyes and smiled with the most beautiful smile. She didn't need to say anything else. Her intercession for my mother and me had so blessed me. I've never forgotten that moment. I realized in a new way the tremendous power of intercessory prayer.

Paul, the Lord's apostle to the Gentile church, often asked others to pray for him. He said, "Don't forget to pray for me" (Ephesians 6:19 MSG). And then he shared his specific requests: "Pray that I'll know what to say and have the courage to say it at the right time, telling the mystery to one and all." Paul also set a profound example of intercessory prayer for the early church. He said, "We give thanks to God, the Father of our Lord Jesus Christ, praying always for you...we have not ceased to pray for you to ask that you may be filled with the knowledge of His will in all spiritual wisdom and understanding...I labor, striving according to His power, which mightily works within me" (Colossians 1:3,9,29). His example of prayer throughout the New Testament demonstrates the priority and necessity of intercessory prayer.

Moses was a master at intercessory prayer. He prayed for God's people even in their darkest hour, when no one else would have prayed for them. The people of Israel had created a gold image of a calf and worshipped it instead of the one true God, who had freed them from the tyranny of Egypt. God said to Moses, "They have quickly turned aside from the way which I commanded them" (Exodus 32:8). Now God's anger was burning against the idolatry of His people, but Moses stepped in as intercessor. Moses "stood in the breach" before God on behalf of the people (Psalm 106:23).

This is such a picture of true intercession. For who ever really deserves such serious entreaty to the one true God? Interceding for others means we plead to God on their behalf. We don't plead because of the worthiness of others to receive our prayers but because of the worthiness of our God, to whom we pray. He is worthy of every prayer we can offer on others' behalf. When He hears and responds, He gets all the glory.

How then can we become intercessors? We can learn how to intercede from the example of Moses. He pleaded for the people using the promises God gave to Abraham, Isaac, and Israel (Exodus 32:11-13). In our best prayers for others, we will always plead the promises of God—who He is, what He does, and what He says. For God honors what He has said in His Word.

I know one lady who prays for others using 3 x 5 cards of Scripture verses. Another keeps Scripture prayer verses in a journal on her computer. When I pray for others, I love to open the pages of the Bible, holding the Scripture in my hands. I often plead God's promises in this way: *Lord, You promise that You will cause all things to work together for good to those who love You and are called according to Your purpose* (Romans 8:28). *Lord, You promise to supply all our needs according to Your riches in glory in Christ Jesus* (Philippians 4:19). And then I like to pray God's Word in this way: *Lord, I pray that You would strengthen my friend, according to the riches of Your glory, with power through Your Spirit in her inner person, so that Christ may dwell in her heart through faith, and that she, being rooted and grounded in love, may be able to comprehend with all the saints what is the breadth and length and height and depth, and to know Your love which surpasses knowledge, that she would be filled with Your fullness* (Ephesians 3:16-19). Praying through Scripture for others is one of my favorite ways to pray for people—and especially for my husband, family, and friends.

Another excellent way to learn the art of intercession is to pray for those in your neighborhood. Prayer-walking takes a proactive approach to intercession. I have another friend who resolved to make a difference in her neighborhood for Christ. Using a map of every home in the neighborhood, she wrote the names of people and families and prayed over every house. She walked her dogs every day in that neighborhood and prayed for every home. As a result, with time, she grew to know and love the people of that neighborhood, and she was able to encourage them to know Christ. She now lives in another part of California, but she is still walking those dogs and praying for her neighbors. Of course, they have no idea she is interceding on their behalf. But they had better get ready for amazing and incredible things to happen, for the Lord loves seeing us take Him seriously and pray.

Another way to intercede for others is to pray for the world. You might be thinking, *How can I pray for the whole world?* The world literally sets the stage for your prayer. We can pray for others as we simply walk through a mall—looking for the lonely man sitting on the bench or the woman taking care of her children. You can pray for one person, one group of people, or one country at a time. Use the newspaper or an online news service to prompt you to pray. Unrest, famine, and poverty are graphically portrayed on almost every page. Always remember the mercy, compassion, and lovingkindness of the Lord. When you grow in intimacy with your Lord, your heart will be burdened with what crushes His heart. You will see everything with His eyes of love, and you will be moved to pray for people you don't even know. If you and I only realized how God responds to our cries on behalf of others, I know we would pray more often and more fervently.

I have many prayer tools that I use in my quiet time. I don't use them all at once, nor do I use them every day. But they are of great help in guiding my prayers for others. Two of my favorites are *Operation World* and *The Global Prayer Digest*. Our church participates in the National Day of Prayer every year, praying for our nation. The Global Day of Prayer is an opportunity to join together with others to pray for the world.

I especially love to use the Adore God in Prayer section of my *Quiet Time Notebook,* devoting pages to family and friends and then recording my prayer requests for them. I find the more specific I am with my requests, the more easily I am able to recognize God's responses to my prayers. Don't forget to write out how He answers your prayers as a confirmation of His faithfulness. George Mueller provides a wonderful example—his prayer requests throughout his life filled more than 3000 pages and resulted in a record of more than 30,000 answers to prayer. Now *that's* an intercessory prayer warrior!

I like to use visual aids in prayer, such as maps, newspapers, or photographs. I put photos of others in the Adore God in Prayer section of my *Quiet Time Notebook.* Those photos help me pray more faithfully for my friends and family. At our ministry headquarters we have a large map on the wall. We add pins to the map when a new area begins a study using one of our books. We pray over that map. I am amazed to see the spread of pins all across it, signifying to us the movement of God in response to our prayers as He reaches people in all parts of the world.

We witness much power when we join together with others and pray in unified, agreeing prayer. Almost every Monday morning, our Quiet Time Ministries staff team gathers in our conference room with our notebooks open to prayer pages and with our pencils in hand. We write out requests for one another and requests for our ministry. And then we pray. We have seen the Lord answer our prayers in amazing ways. One of the key staff members in our ministry underwent extensive chemotherapy for lymphoma. We prayed that the Lord would keep her strong throughout her treatment. Amazingly, she never missed a day of ministry work and was able to continue to teach, write articles, and speak at conferences.

One of the most important ways to intercede for others is to pray for those who are sick and to ask the Lord for their healing. James speaks of the importance of praying for those who are sick and anointing them with oil in the name of the Lord (James 5:14-16). I am so thankful for my friend Pastor Jim Smoke, who often prays for those who are suffering from pain and illness. More than once, he has invited me to go with him to pray for someone.

I remember the day we went to see Sue, one of the women in our ministry, who was dying. What a precious time of prayer we had with her. Within days, she was in heaven with the Lord. And I remember going with Jim to pray for a man battling cancer. I watched Jim take some oil from Israel and use it to draw a cross on the man's forehead. Then we prayed together for his strength and healing. I have learned that God always answers our prayers but not necessarily in the ways we might desire. Sometimes He heals and prolongs physical life on earth. Other times He gives what I call "ultimate healing" and brings a person to heaven, face-to-face with Him.

I often feel that when we intercede, we are like the friends of Moses who held up his hands to gain the victory over the Amalekites (Exodus 17:12). Moses became weary and fatigued and could no longer hold up his arms. As his arms began to fall, the people of Israel began to lose the battle. Aaron and Hur rushed to his side and held up his arms, keeping his hands steady until the sun went down. As a result, Joshua defeated the Amalekites. This is a wonderful picture of intercessory prayer, where we pray diligently and persistently for those in our lives who have needs requiring the Lord's help.

My most intimate experiences of intercessory prayer occur when the Lord brings someone to my mind and compels me to drop everything and pray for that person. Several years ago during the Christmas holidays, He brought a long-lost friend to my mind, and I began praying. That friend was so much on my heart and mind that I e-mailed others, made phone calls, and researched online, trying to find out where she lived so I could call her. I finally found her contact information and made the call. Oh, how glad I am that I listened to the Lord! Connecting with each other again has renewed a friendship that encourages our walk with the Lord. As a result, we have once again become very close, praying for one another in our walk with Christ.

I was once awakened suddenly in the middle of the night with thoughts of my brother coming to mind. Praying, I fell asleep again. I awoke again at four o'clock and decided to get up. In my quiet time I prayed earnestly for my brother, and his entire family. I received an urgent call a couple of hours later from my brother telling me of a water main break flooding their house. The flooding had mysteriously stopped sometime during the night. Of course, we don't know when the water stopped, but I wonder if it happened when I began earnestly praying, enlisting the aid of my Father in heaven, who sees all and is all-powerful.

I love knowing that God responds to the prayers of His people! God's response to Daniel's prayers for his people has often encouraged me to pray. The angel Gabriel came to Daniel and told him that God issued His command of response at the beginning of Daniel's supplications. And this may be true for us. Just imagine—we can have the ear of our God as we begin to pray. He issues commands in response to our prayers as we intercede for others.

Elizabeth Alves awoke late one night, at once seeing the face of her cousin Mike in her mind. She dropped to her knees and cried out, "God, don't let Mike move! Keep him still, Lord! Keep him still! Oh God, please don't let him move! Hold him, Lord! Hold him!" Some time later she was compelled to pray, "Get him up, Lord! Get him to run!" She continued to pray, yet wondered why she was so suddenly and profoundly burdened for this young man. A month later she received the answer.

Mike was a pilot, serving in Vietnam. He had been shot down and fell into a bush. He wrote, "It felt like I was pinned down. I felt like somebody was sitting on me. The Vietcong came and were unknowingly standing on my pant leg while looking up at my parachute in the tree. They turned around and began to slash the bushes with their bayonets. It looked safe, so I started to get up and was about to run when once again I fell into the bush as though someone were pushing me. I laid there for a couple of minutes when suddenly I had an impulse to get up and run. I heard a helicopter so I sprinted through the wooded area, following the direction of the noise, to an open space where I was whisked off to safety. The helicopter crew said they came in response to my beeper. And yet, it had not been working when I was shot down."[1]

Never underestimate the power of God in response to your intercessory prayers on behalf of another. And when God brings someone to your mind, the greatest thing you do is pray.

Because You Prayed

Because you prayed,
God touched our weary bodies with His power,
And gave us strength for many a trying hour
In which we might have faltered
Had not you, our intercessors,
Faithful been and true.

Because you prayed;
God touched our eager fingers with His skill,
Enabling us to do His blessed will.
With scalpel, suture, bandage—better still
He healed the sick and wounded, cured the ill.

Because you prayed,
God touched our lips with coals from altar fire,
Gave Spirit fullness, and did so inspire
That when we spoke, sin-blinded souls did see,
Sin's chains were broken;
Captives were made free.

Because you prayed,
The dwellers in the dark have found the Light;
The glad good news has banished heathen night;
The message of the cross, so long delayed,
Has brought them life at last
Because you prayed![2]

CHARLES B. BOWSER

DATE:

KEY VERSE: "Pray for one another" (James 5:16).

FOR FURTHER THOUGHT: What is the most important truth you have learned about intercessory prayer? Who is on your heart to pray for right now? Draw near to the Father and pray for them.

MY RESPONSE:

Day Twenty-Seven

REVIVAL PRAYER

The eyes of the LORD move to and fro
throughout the earth that He may strongly
support those whose heart is completely His.

2 CHRONICLES 16:9

God is looking for prayer warriors for revival. He told Ezekiel, "I searched for a man among them who would build up the wall and stand in the gap before Me for the land, so that I would not destroy it; but I found no one" (Ezekiel 22:30). When we pray on behalf of churches, lands, and nations, we can know that God is pleased. He honors those prayers with His attention and His powerful response. And today's verse reminds us, "The eyes of the LORD move to and fro throughout the earth that He may strongly support those whose heart is completely His." The Hebrew word translated "support" is *chazaq* (to make strong or strengthen), but the key phrase is "whose heart is completely His." If we will first give ourselves to the Lord and then plead with Him on behalf of a godless, heartsick, and complacent people, we will have His ear. This kind of intercessory prayer is what I call revival prayer.

Revival prayer is greatly desired by God when groups of people or nations are in dire trouble. Used over a dozen times in the Psalms alone, the Hebrew word translated "revive" is *chayah* and means literally to be restored to life. Solomon, while dedicating the newly built temple to God, asked God to "hear…from heaven" and forgive the people if they sinned against Him (2 Chronicles 6:21-27). The Lord responded to Solomon at night when he was alone. And that is frequently how God responds—He meets the one alone whose ear is open to hear what He has to say. The Lord said, "[If] my people who are called by my name humble themselves and pray and seek My face and turn from their wicked ways, then will I hear from heaven, will forgive their sin and heal their land" (2 Chronicles 7:14). God is looking for men and women who will pray with humility, passion, devotion, repentance, and confession.

Revival prayer is an extraordinary type of prayer. Extraordinary prayer is rarely practiced in this day and age, for it is strategic and requires great commitment. But it gains the ear of God. J. Edwin Orr, the leading expert on revivals in the twentieth century, spoke of this kind of extraordinary prayer in his message "The Role of Prayer in Spiritual Awakening":

> What do we mean by extraordinary prayer? We share ordinary prayer in regular worship services, before meals, and the like. But when people are found getting up at six in the morning to pray, or having a half night of prayer until midnight, or giving up their lunch time to pray at noonday prayer meetings, that is extraordinary prayer. It must be united and concerted.

Revival prayer is a strategic and purposeful pleading with God to intervene in the affairs of men and nations. Orr said, "There has never been a spiritual awakening in any country or locality that did not begin in united prayer." God is looking for people who will ask Him to move powerfully in the hearts of others.

Following the Second Great Awakening and the death of John Wesley, spiritual conditions deteriorated in Europe and especially in the United States. America was deeply divided over the issue of slavery, and the pursuit of money and material possessions became the top priority for many people. In September 1857, Jeremiah Lanphier advertised a weekly prayer meeting for businessmen at noon in the upper room of the Dutch Reformed Church Consistory Building in Manhattan. Only six men responded out of a population of a million. The following week there were 14, then 23, and then they decided to meet every day to pray. So many men began to meet daily for prayer that they had to relocate frequently due to lack of space. By February of 1858, every public hall and church in downtown New York was filled with those who met for daily prayer.

Horace Greeley, a famous news editor, sent a man by horse and buggy to as many meetings as possible one day to see how many men were praying. He could get to only 12 meetings in one hour, but he counted 6100 men. J. Edwin Orr described what happened as a result:

> Then a landslide of prayer began, which overflowed to the churches in the evenings. People began to be converted, ten thousand a week in New York City alone. The movement spread throughout New England, the church bells bringing people to prayer at eight in the morning, twelve noon, and six in the evening. The revival raced up the Hudson and down the Mohawk, where the Baptists, for example, had so many people to baptize that they went down to the river, cut a big hole in the ice, and baptized them in the cold water. When Baptists do that they are really on fire![1]

Can God do again what He has done in the past? Yes! I believe He can and will do even more than what we can ask or imagine, according to the power that is at work in us (Ephesians 3:20-21). I believe He is looking for those who will join together in a united concert of strategic, purposeful, pleading prayer on behalf of people and nations. If you knew you instantly had the ear of God, what would you say to Him? What would you ask of Him? I would ask for a huge revival in the land. I would like to see those dry bones that Ezekiel saw in the valley come to life (Ezekiel 37:1-14). God told Ezekiel, "I will put My Spirit within you and you will come to life." One of my favorite prayers is taken from Isaiah 64:1: Tear open the skies and come down to earth so that the mountains will tremble before you" (NCV). Your cry becomes like the psalmists: "I waited patiently for the LORD; and He inclined to me and heard my cry" (Psalm 40:1).

Your prayers will require perseverance. Spurgeon says, "Perseverance in prayer is necessary to prevalence in prayer."[2] Then God comes through the heavens, and His Spirit moves in a powerful way among people. You would see dry bones come to life.

Revival prayer changes lives. When God's people were allowed to return to Jerusalem with Ezra, they sinned against God and intermarried with the people of the lands (Ezra 9:1-2). God's people were to be holy and separate, pure and distinct, unstained by the sinful practices of those around them. Ezra, the revival prayer warrior, responded with great dismay, as do all who are truly burdened with what presses in on God's heart. So he tore his garments, pulled hair from his head and beard, and sat down appalled (Ezra 9:3). His fierce reaction so impressed the people of Israel that they trembled. In the evening, with a torn robe, Ezra fell on his knees, stretched out his hands to God, and prayed a revival prayer. He began by saying, "O my God, I am ashamed and embarrassed to lift up my face to You, my God, for our iniquities have risen above our heads and our guilt has grown even to the heavens" (Ezra 9:6). What a powerful way to begin a prayer! He continued begging God for mercy and forgiveness. His prayer was so effective that all the people gathered around him and wept with bitterness. And friend, when hearts begin to break over sin, true revival has begun. Brokenness leads to repentance. And repentance leads to revival. Peter said, "Therefore, repent and return, so that your sins may be wiped away, in order that times of refreshing may come from the presence of the Lord" (Acts 3:19). Ezra was an instrument of revival used by God to turn the people of God back to the Lord.

You may be wondering, *Could God use me like Ezra in this generation?* I believe God is waiting for us to pray and ask Him for a mighty movement of the Holy Spirit that sweeps through churches among people and creates a powerful fire of revival. God is looking for those who will see sin the way Ezra saw it—as an offense against the one true God whose compassions and mercies have never failed. Do you see what God sees? Do you notice that God's house is no longer a house of prayer (Matthew 21:13)? Do you sense that there is more of the world influencing the church than the church impacting the world (1 John 2:15)? Are you appalled at the utter godlessness of the world, displayed in the media for all to see? Do you sense our world becoming increasingly similar to Sodom and Gomorrah? If I had a beard I would tear it out, just as Ezra did.

What about you? And what about me? Are we appalled when God convicts us of our own sin? Are we brokenhearted when we become numb to things that would have pricked our hearts on another day? We never want it to be said of us, "You have left your first love" (Revelation 2:4). I ask God to keep me tender and softhearted so I can draw near and enjoy unbroken, joyous fellowship with Him.

Our prayers for revival are even more effective when we fast and pray with others in united prayer. Jesus assumed that His disciples would fast and pray (Matthew 6:5-6,16; 9:15). Dr. Bill Bright, cofounder of Campus Crusade for Christ, said, "The power of fasting as it relates to prayer is the spiritual atomic bomb that our Lord has given us to destroy the strongholds of evil and usher in a great revival and spiritual harvest around the world." In a fast, believers voluntarily choose to go without food or something else important to their lives for a set period of time in order to seek the face of God, drawing near to Him in humility and reverence. You can fast from many different things, including food, speech, social interaction, television, or computers. Fasts are effective means to focus your attention on God and His Word, enabling you to fervently pray for needs in your life and in the lives of others.

When we pray with others in agreement, we put the enemy into the danger zone. Jesus promises, "If two of you agree on earth about anything that they may ask, it shall be done for them by My Father who is in heaven" (Matthew 18:19). The early church knew this secret, for they prayed "with one accord" (Acts 4:24), and we are told that "when they had prayed, the place where they had gathered together was shaken, and they were all filled with the Holy Spirit and began to speak the word of God with boldness" (Acts 4:31). One of the most powerful steps you can take in your life of prayer is to find a prayer partner or a group of prayer partners to meet with on a regular basis. Pray for each other and for personal and corporate revival. Keep a list of all that you are bringing to the throne of God, for as God answers, you will rejoice in the encouragement of His mighty power in response to your prayers.

I remember the first time I met with others to pray. I was standing in a circle in a small room with ten other people, all of whom were staff members with Campus Crusade at Arizona State University. I guess I hadn't really realized what was going to happen. Kent started to pray, and I suddenly realized that this prayer would move around the circle. I had never prayed out loud. I thought, *Oh no, what am I going to do? What am I going to say?* I knew I couldn't run or blend into the wall, so I stood my ground, remaining as quiet as possible. I was so quiet that when the person next to me finished her prayer, I said nothing, terrified and speechless. Finally, after some awkward moments of silence, the person on my other side resumed the chain of prayer, and I was off the hook.

On my way home that night I thought, *I'll never be able to pray such eloquent prayers to the Lord in the presence of others.* However, I kept going to these prayer sessions because I sensed the power of God in our united, strategic, purposeful prayer. We had seen Him answer our prayers in extraordinary ways. And that greatly encouraged me. Well, one day, I mustered up the courage and prayed out loud. At first I was self-conscious, but soon I focused on the Lord and not my words, and the prayer flowed. With time, I couldn't get enough and began to join in with every prayer group I could find. When you pray with others, you will experience an excitement that will increase your faith as together you believe God will make extraordinary responses. Revive us again, O Lord!

DATE:

KEY VERSE: "The eyes of the LORD move to and fro throughout the earth that He may strongly support those whose heart is completely His" (2 Chronicles 16:9).

FOR FURTHER THOUGHT: How is your heart burdened for revival? Write a prayer to the Lord, expressing all that is on your heart. Think about joining with one or more friends as prayer partners for revival and needs in your life.

MY RESPONSE:

Day Twenty-Eight

EFFECTIVE PRAYER

The effective prayer of a righteous
man can accomplish much.

JAMES 5:16

Pleading the promises of God unleashes a tremendous dynamic power and yields amazing results. James' statement of encouragement is at once understated and profound: "The effective prayer of a righteous man can accomplish much." James explained this declaration with the faithful prayer of Elijah, the perfect example, for he was a man just like us. Friends, the men and women of the Bible were ordinary people who connected in prayer with the one true God, extraordinary Creator, and sovereign Lord and Savior. Never become overwhelmed by your own inadequacy, but instead be consumed with the all-sufficiency of your Lord. Elijah prayed to stop the rain for three years, and God answered, causing a drought in the land. After three years, the Lord came to Elijah and said He was going to make it rain, again in answer to Elijah's prayers. Elijah's prayers were so effective that they even impacted the weather report. That's effective prayer!

What is effective prayer? I like Matthew Henry's commentary on James 5:16, which amplifies and paraphrases this verse:

And when a righteous person, a true believer, justified in Christ, and by his grace walking before God in holy obedience, presents an effectual fervent prayer, wrought in his heart by the power of the Holy Spirit, raising holy affections and believing expectations and so leading earnestly to plead the promises of God at his mercy-seat, it avails much.[1]

Effective prayer will increase your faith in God and your passion for Christ. The Greek word translated "effective" is *energeo,* which means to put forth power or produce an effect. How can our prayers be so effective that they accomplish much? James says we must be righteous. We learn from James that who we are and how we live is of the utmost importance to our prayers. The Greek word translated "righteous" is *dikaios* and means that our way of life is to be consistent with who we are in Christ. A righteous man is one who is earnest, heartfelt, and virtuous, keeping the commands of God. We live by God's standard, not our own. Elijah is an example of a righteous man whose prayer was effective. Elijah was not merely a talker; he was a walker—he walked with God. When God spoke, Elijah listened and obeyed. He knew who God was and what He could accomplish, and that prompted boldness in his prayers to God.

The lesson for us is to pay attention to who we are and how we live. Growing spiritually in our relationship with God is of paramount importance in becoming effective in our prayers. When we resolve to walk with God, we place our quiet time as a top priority. The Bible is our handbook for life. We must know it well and dearly love every verse. It's not mere coincidence that James is the one who said, "But prove yourselves doers of the word, and not merely hearers who delude themselves" (James 1:22).

Our time alone with God is where we read and hear God's Word. But where will we go from there? Will we listen? Will we talk with God? Will we live by faith? Will we take God at His Word? These questions strike at the heart of effective prayers. For God does not look at the outward appearance but at the heart (1 Samuel 16:7). The passion coming from a heart that dares to draw near and walk intimately with God, day by day and moment by moment, becomes the fabric and substance of one's life. This is the impetus driving effective prayer. Such people truly live in the audience of God. And they are not afraid to storm the doors of heaven and boldly approach their God. For they have walked with Him before and are walking with Him still. Such hearts know what God can do. Knowing He is the God who can do anything, they dream big, exercise their faith, believe God, and ask for the impossible—such as moving mountains (Mark 11:23-24), prolonging the day (Joshua 10:12-14), and stopping the rain (James 5:17-18).

And what then can such effective prayers accomplish? James tells us: "much." In this single word, James declares the great power of walking and talking with God. The *Translator's New Testament* puts it this way: "The good man's prayer is very powerful because God is at work in it." The power of prayer is the power of God. Prayer has no power without the power of God. Effective prayers grasp hold of God and His power. John Maxwell says, "The 'detonator' that churches lack today is prayer. It has the power to ignite the dynamite of the Gospel and powerfully shake the world."

In Goa, India, a mission reported that despite numerous attempts, they had been able to plant only eight house churches over a period of 20 years. A team of intercessors from Brazil traveled to Goa and prayed for a year. They did not witness, distribute printed materials, or engage in any kind of church planting. They simply prayed. Two months after the intercessors left, 18 new house churches were planted in a city that was no longer resistant to the gospel.

Oh, how incredible the power of God is for those who go through life on their knees. Many men and women have discovered the secret of marching ahead in life on their knees. Such was the case for "Gypsy" Smith, an evangelist in Great Britain and the United States in the early 1900s. As a young boy, he longed for the conversion of his uncle Rodney. And yet in the strict Gypsy culture, children could not address elders unless spoken to first. One day, his uncle noticed Gypsy's worn trousers. "Laddie," said Uncle Rodney, "how do you account for the fact that the knees of your trousers have worn nearly through, while the rest of the suit is almost like new?"

"I have worn the knees through praying for you, Uncle Rodney." And then he added tearfully, "I want so much to have God make you a Christian!" Uncle Rodney put his arm around Gypsy and a few moments later fell on his knees and confessed Christ as his Savior.

Phillips Brooks, author and pastor in the late1800s, confessed, "Prayer is not conquering God's reluctance, but laying hold of God's willingness." The "much" that effective prayers can accomplish includes your deepest and greatest needs. What do you want? What secret longing in your heart have you tried to cover up for so long? Lay it all out before the Lord. Don't ever settle for sitting on the sidelines with God. Instead, draw near and commune with Him. Storm the doors of heaven with every want, every need, every burden, every care. Enter the throne room of your Father. He is waiting for you even now.

DATE:

KEY VERSE: "The effective prayer of a righteous man can accomplish much" (James 5:16).

FOR FURTHER THOUGHT: What do you need from God, dear friend? Do you walk with Him day by day? Do you storm the doors of heaven, bold in your prayers, because you know what it is to walk and talk with Him each day? Will you resolve anew to walk with your Lord and live by what He says in His Word? And then, will you pray?

MY RESPONSE:

THE GLORY OF PRAYER

They will see His face.

REVELATION 22:4

Your final glory of prayer is to see God face-to-face. Yes, someday you will see the Lord directly in heaven. The view of heaven given to John on Patmos points toward our firsthand experience of seeing the face of the Lord. He says, "There will no longer be any curse; and the throne of God and of the Lamb will be in it, and His bond-servants will serve Him; they will see His face, and His name will be on their foreheads" (Revelation 22:3-4). And then, John tells us, "We will see Him just as He is" (1 John 3:2).

Fanny Crosby, the American poet of the late 1800s who wrote the words to more than 8000 hymns, was blind from birth. One time a preacher sympathetically remarked, "I think it is a great pity that the Master did not give you sight when He showered so many gifts upon you."

She replied quickly, "Do you know that if at birth I had been able to make one petition, it would have been that I should be born blind?"

"Why?" asked the surprised clergyman.

"Because when I get to heaven, the first face that shall ever gladden my sight will be that of my Savior." Perhaps our prayerful longing for the face of Jesus is no better expressed than by Fanny herself:

> Someday my earthly house will fall.
> I cannot tell how soon 'twill be;
> But this I know—my All In All
> Has now a place in heaven for me.
> And I shall see Him face to face,
> And tell the story—saved by grace.

At the turn of the twentieth century, Lettie and Charles Cowman served as missionaries in the Orient at the Bible Training Institute, their faithful service placing the Word of God in 10,300,000 homes. Mrs. Cowman describes those times as "blessed days." Then, out of the blue, in the midst of a wonderful missionary service, Charles suffered a devastating stroke. Lettie described the six long years that followed as "the darkest hour that ever swept a human life."[1]

These dire circumstances might have sent Charles into anger, depression, and mental collapse. But Lettie Cowman records that God gave Charles a great faith and enabled him to praise triumphantly. She explains the glory of prayer he discovered:

> If God were to give him songs in the night, He must first make it night. The refining fires never raged beyond His control. The billows, which in their approach threatened to submerge him as they came in, lifted him up to heaven for which he was bound. All the waves were crested with God's benediction. God answered his prayer in His own way, permitting him to be shut in with Himself that he might find the treasures of darkness, delivering him with such a mighty hand that he was glad that the tempest arose, for the furious winds and tumbling seas reveal to him *what manner of man is this.*

Regardless of how dark the day grows, we may triumph in faith and walk and talk with God in passionate prayer. This is the true glory of prayer.

Mrs. Cowman penned this untitled poem almost as an afterthought in *Springs in the Valley,* remembering her husband's final days:

> The way was long, and the shadows spread far as the eye
>   could see.
> I stretched my hands to a human Christ, who walked
>   through the night with me.
> Out of the darkness we came at last, our feet on the dawn-
>   warm sod.
> And I knew by the light in His wondrous eye, that I
>   walked with the Son of God.[2]

Do you know that you walk with the Son of God? Perhaps you too have had what you thought were the best and blessed years, what you might even call your bright, shining, glory years. And maybe now the light seems dim because of the darkness of trial or suffering. Remember, God is faithful to give you treasures of darkness and songs in the night (Psalm 77:6; Isaiah 45:3). Your greatest glory is even now—and yet to come!

The face of the Lord is seen now dimly "through a mirror," but then face-to-face (1 Corinthians 13:12). That mirror includes the Bible, the Word of God itself (James 1:22-25). Those who know their Bible well see His face most clearly, with sharp spiritual vision. And those who have the best vision pray the best, with passion and power. Indeed, great revivals have been borne out of prayers with open Bibles. George Whitefield prayed on his knees with his open Bible. May it be also with you. Our life of passionate prayer is only a brief moment when compared to our life in eternity. Let us agree together to spend that life well. May we walk and talk with God in passionate prayer all our days on earth.

I often think about the day I will step from time into eternity and see my Lord face-to-face. I will finally look into the eyes of the one I've been walking and talking with all of these days on earth. I want my gaze into His face to be a knowing look, an exchange between my Lord and me of familiarity and even more—a moment of intimacy. I don't want it to be a first experience, but a part of my ongoing relationship with Him that began during my brief stay on earth. I want to fall into His arms and be able to say, "Lord, I'm here. I'm home—finally, always, and forever. I love You more now than ever before."

Oh, sometimes my faith sees Jesus coming o'er the stormy sea.

And the waves are stilled, the raging tempest past;

Then the clouds return again, clouds of care and grief and
pain,

And the sweetness of His presence does not last.

But some day I'll bide with Him where no storm His face
shall dim—

He who loves me and who saves me by His grace.

Here I walk by faith, not sight; but I'm walking toward the
light,

And—what glory when I see Him face to face![3]

DATE:

KEY VERSE: "They will see His face" (Revelation 22:4).

FOR FURTHER THOUGHT: Think about the race the Lord has set before you today. What will it take for you to run your race and finish well? What does seeing the Lord's face when you step from time into eternity mean to you? Close your time today by writing a prayer, expressing all that is on your heart.

MY RESPONSE:

Day Thirty

QUIET TIME WEEK FIVE: THE POWER OF PRAYER

Grace and peace be multiplied to you in the
knowledge of God and of Jesus our Lord;
seeing that His divine power has granted to
us everything pertaining to life and godliness,
through the true knowledge of Him who
called us by His own glory and excellence.

2 PETER 1:2-3

PREPARE YOUR HEART

People often asked Billy Graham, "What was the secret of your evangelistic crusades?"

He replied, "There are three secrets. Prayer. Prayer. Prayer."[1]

Oh, what power there is in prayer, for your prayers bring you into contact with the living God. When you pray, you enter into the throne room of God Himself. And your prayers unleash the power of God into your life, into the lives of those around you, and on into the world. A.W. Tozer said, "All of the advertising we can do will never equal the interest and participation in the things of God resulting from the gracious answers to the prayers of faith generated by the Holy Spirit."[2] What is the secret to a great move of God in your life and your ministry? Prayer.

You have spent the last 29 days thinking about prayer and how to discover the power of talking with God. You have looked at why we pray, how to pray, examples of prayer, and many ideas for your life of prayer. Today, in your last day of this 30-day journey, you are going to think about the great and mighty power of God, the one to whom you pray. Ask God to speak to you as you draw near and open the pages of His Word.

READ AND STUDY GOD'S WORD

1. God is all-powerful and enough for everything you face in life. Peter encourages us that "His divine power has granted to us everything pertaining to life and godliness." His power gives us everything we need in life. In Mark 14:63, Jesus describes Himself as sitting at the right hand of power. God Himself is power. The word for "power" is *dunamis* and points to a power that makes us able and capable. God's power enables us to achieve God's will and accomplish His work. If we want to do what God has asked us to do, we need to run to Him for strength and power. Read Acts 1:8 and record what you learn about the power of God.

2. How powerful is God? Look at the following verses and write out everything you learn about the power of God and what God can do.

Genesis 1:1

Exodus 14:21-22

Acts 4:33

1 Corinthians 1:18

2 Corinthians 4:7

2 Corinthians 12:9

1 Peter 1:3-6

2 Peter 1:2-3

Revelation 19:1

3. What have you learned about God's power that encourages you to cry out to God in prayer for help in your time of need?

ADORE GOD IN PRAYER

Think back over the last 30 days and all you have learned about prayer. Ask the Lord to take what you have learned and apply it to your life in such a meaningful way that you will, day by day, walk and talk with Him.

YIELD YOURSELF TO GOD

> I want to tell you a growing conviction with me, and that is that as we obey the leadings of the Spirit of God, we enable God to answer the prayers of other people. I mean that our lives, my life is the answer to someone's prayer, prayed perhaps centuries ago…I have the unspeakable knowledge that my life is the answer to prayers, and that God is blessing me and making me a blessing entirely of His sovereign grace and nothing to do with my merits, saving as I am bold enough to trust His leading and not the dictates of my own wisdom and common sense.[3]
>
> OSWALD CHAMBERS

> Prayer is a powerful thing. "Prayer has already divided seas and rolled up flowing rivers, it has made flinty rocks gush into fountains, it has quenched flames of fire, it has muzzled lions, disarmed vipers and poisons, it has marshaled the stars against the wicked, it has stopped the course of the moon and arrested the sun in its race, it has burst open iron gates and recalled souls from eternity, it has conquered the strongest devils and commanded legions of angels down from heaven. Prayer has bridled and chained the raging passions of men and destroyed vast armies of proud, daring, blustering atheists. Prayer has brought one man from the bottom of the sea and carried another in a chariot of fire to heaven." That is not mere hyperbole, that is historical fact. Prayer has done a great many other things as well. It is an awesome, mighty force in the world of men.[4]
>
> RAY STEDMAN

ENJOY HIS PRESENCE

Turn back to day 1 and read what you wrote in your letter to the Lord. As you think about this 30-day journey about your life of prayer, summarize in a few sentences the most important truths you have learned. What was your favorite day of reading and why? How will this journey make a difference in your life, and what will you carry with you? And finally, what is your greatest prayer?

REST IN HIS LOVE

"But we have this treasure in earthen vessels, so that the surpassing greatness of the power will be of God and not from ourselves" (2 Corinthians 4:7).

Notes—Week Five

APPENDIXES

DISCUSSION QUESTIONS

These questions are for people who share this 30-day journey together. This book is a great tool for talking together about prayer. It also provides for a great 30-day preparation for one of the books of quiet times available from Quiet Time Ministries. God bless you as you help others discover the joy of passionate prayer.

Introduction

Use the introduction week to meet those in your group, hand out copies of this book, familiarize everyone with the topic of passionate prayer, and play the introduction message (if you are using the weekly DVD messages for *Passionate Prayer*). Begin your group time by asking, "What brought you to this 30-day journey? How did you hear about it?" Allow everyone to share. Then pass out the books and show those in your group how each week is organized, with a quiet time as the sixth day. Show your group all the information in appendix 2. Tell them about the websites www.passionate prayerbook.com, www.quiettime.org, and www.myquiettime.com as well as the Quiet Time Café message board at www.quiettimecafe.com, where they can share insights online with others. Then describe how you will structure each week's meeting. You may want to use a sign-up sheet for snacks. Close in prayer.

Week One: Perspective for Your Life of Prayer

DAY 1: When You Hear His Music

1. Begin your time together in prayer.

2. As you lead your group through a discussion of each day, you may want to have someone read the verse at the beginning of each day. Then, as you begin this discussion, ask your group to share what it meant to them to spend daily time this last week thinking about prayer.

3. What meant the most to you in the introduction?

4. How does the metaphor of music help you understand prayer?

5. After reading through all the days in this first week, how would you define prayer?

DAY 2: The Rhythm of the Music

1. In day 2 you read that the rhythm of your life will determine your ability to pray. What does that mean?

2. Why is it so difficult to take time, slow down, and pray?

3. How can we slow down and take time alone with God? What will help us do that in our lives?

4. Where are you in your own journey of prayer?

DAY 3: The Composer of the Music

1. What did you learn about God in day 3?

2. What is His relationship to your prayers?

3. How does God help you pray?

DAY 4: Your Song to the Lord

1. Why is prayer like a song you sing to the Lord?

2. Why do we pray? What did you learn in day 4 about the reasons for prayer?

3. Why do you think God might be shocked when we do not pray?

4. What is your favorite truth from day 4 about prayer?

5. What did you learn from the story about D.L. Moody?

DAY 5: When You Finally Sing

1. How does prayer change us?

2. What was your favorite quote or story from day 5?

DAY 6: The Privilege of Prayer Quiet Time

1. On day 6 you had the opportunity to experience a quiet time on the privilege of prayer. Why is prayer such a privilege?

2. What did you learn from your study in the Word of God on prayer?

3. What quote, verse, or insight encouraged you the most this week?

Week Two: A Plan for Your Life of Prayer

DAY 7: Your Prayer Growth Plan

1. Introduce today's discussion with a quick review of what you discussed last week. This will be of special benefit to those who are just joining your group. You might review by sharing what prayer is—walking and talking with God. You might share how prayer is like the song we sing in response to the music of the Word of God. As you lead your group

through a discussion of each day in week 2, you may want to have someone read the verse at the beginning of each day.

2. In day 7 we looked at a prayer growth plan. Why do you think we need a prayer growth plan?

3. Describe the prayer growth plan. What was your favorite part of the prayer growth plan, and what are you looking forward to learning?

4. Have you ever written out your prayer requests in a prayer journal or notebook? If so, how did that help you in your life of prayer?

DAY 8: Learning to Talk with God

1. How has God already initiated an ongoing conversation with you?

2. What kinds of prayers can we write in our prayer journal?

3. Why is using Scripture such a powerful way to pray? What portions of the Bible are especially conducive to prayer?

4. What will help us slow down and listen to God?

5. What did you learn about the importance of thanking God from the story of Corrie and Betsie ten Boom?

DAY 9: Learning from Others

1. In day 9 you thought about the value of learning from others in your life of prayer. In what ways can you learn from others?

2. What is one of your favorite books on prayer?

3. How can selectively adding books to your prayer growth plan help you grow in prayer?

4. What new book would you like to read on prayer after *Passionate Prayer?*

DAY 10: Your Adventure in Prayer

1. Describe your own adventure in prayer. What is the most important thing you've learned about prayer in the last few years?

2. What idea or prayer resource from day 10 would you like to try in your own life of prayer?

DAY 11: Your Adventure in Knowing God

1. How does knowing who God is, what He does, and what He says help in your life of prayer?

2. What quality about God helps you pray the most? What is it about Him that encourages you to draw near and pray?

DAY 12: The Partnership of Prayer Quiet Time

1. In your quiet time on day 12, you learned that prayer is to occur in the context of an intimate relationship with the Lord. How does this help in motivating you to pray?

2. What is most significant to you in the words of Jesus in John 17?

3. What was your favorite quote in the quiet time in day 12?

4. What was your favorite insight, quote, or verse from your reading and study this week?

5. What have you thought about most this week as you have engaged in this 30-day journey of prayer?

Week Three: Patterns for Your Life of Prayer

DAY 13: The Prayer Life of Hannah

1. In the last two weeks we have been talking about prayer and how we can grow in our life of prayer. We have seen that prayer is simply walking and talking with God in the context of our intimate relationship with Him. Last week we talked

about the importance of having a prayer growth plan. And we learned about using a prayer journal, praying Scripture, listening to God, thanking the Lord, learning from others through their quotes and books, keeping track of our adventure in prayer, and engaging in the adventure of knowing God. As we begin today, what is the most important thing you've learned so far in this 30-day journey of passionate prayer? (As you lead your group through a discussion of each day in week 3, you may want to have someone read the verse at the beginning of each day.)

2. In day 13 you looked at the life of Hannah. Why is she such an example for us in prayer? What did you learn from her for your own life of prayer?

3. What was your favorite phrase or sentence in the quote by Spurgeon?

DAY 14: The Prayer Life of Nehemiah

1. In day 14 we looked at the example of Nehemiah. What did you learn from him?

2. Why was Nehemiah's prayer so extraordinary?

3. How can our prayers impact thousands?

DAY 15: The Prayer Life of Daniel

1. What did you learn from the example of Daniel?

2. Why does the church need Daniels in this day?

3. What will it take to establish a life of prayer that would convict us if praying were illegal, as it was for a time in Daniel's life?

4. What was your favorite example, quote, or story in day 15?

DAY 16: The Prayer Life of Jesus

1. Why is Jesus our greatest example in prayer?

2. What did Jesus teach about prayer that means the most to you today?

3. What is your favorite part of the Lord's Prayer?

4. How does Jesus' life show us that prayer is more than making requests?

5. How does the example of Jesus show you how essential prayer is to your life?

DAY 17: The Prayer Life of Paul

1. How does Paul encourage us in our lives of prayer?

2. What can we learn from Paul's prayers that can help us know what to pray?

3. How did the story of Dr. Helen Roseveare encourage you in your life of prayer?

DAY 18: The Privacy of Prayer Quiet Time

1. In day 18, you spent time with the Lord, looking at the secret, private nature of prayer in the audience of God. Why was this private prayer in secret with God such a contrast to the prayers of the Pharisees?

2. What do Jesus' words in Matthew 6:1-8 teach us about prayer?

3. How did Jesus model this kind of prayer in His own life? What do you learn from His life of prayer?

4. What was your favorite quote from your quiet time on day 18?

5. What was the most important idea or truth you learned this week in your journey on prayer?

Week Four: Promises for Your Life of Prayer

DAY 19: The Great Response of God

1. We have been looking these last four weeks at prayer and what it means to walk and talk with God. This week we looked at promises for your life of prayer. (As you lead your group through a discussion of each day in week 4, you may want to have someone read the verse at the beginning of each day.)

2. As you spent time this week thinking about God's promises, what was the most important thing you learned? How did God speak to you this week?

3. How do promises from God help us in our life of prayer?

4. When you are in trouble, how does the promise in Psalm 34:17 encourage you to pray?

5. What encouraged you the most from day 19?

DAY 20: The Great Surprise of God

1. In day 20 you learned God's phone number, Jeremiah 33:3. How does this promise encourage us to pray?

2. Why is spiritual vision so important in the Christian life?

3. How did the life of George Mueller encourage you?

4. What difference do you think it would make if people would set aside the many things for the one thing, draw near to God, and get their ideas from Him with a renewed vision and a revived heart?

DAY 21: The Great Goodness of God

1. In day 21 you looked at a promise of the goodness of God. Why is trusting in God's goodness so important when we pray?

2. What stood out to you the most about the goodness of God?

3. Why do we struggle at times with the goodness of God?

4. What was your favorite story, example, or quote on the goodness of God?

DAY 22: The Great Help of God

1. How does God help us in prayer?

2. Describe the ways the Holy Spirit helps us in prayer.

3. What is your greatest need in prayer right now? How do you need the help of the Holy Spirit?

DAY 23: The Great Peace of God

1. Day 23 begins with the statement, "Prayer is God's prescription for a troubled heart." How does prayer help you when you are in trouble?

2. What did you learn from the example of Renée Bondi?

3. Why is prayer important even though God already knows our need?

DAY 24: The Particulars of Prayer Quiet Time

1. What important truths did you learn about prayer from the verses in your quiet time?

2. If you could ask God for anything, what would you ask?

3. What was the most important truth you learned from your quiet time?

4. Was there a favorite verse, quote, or insight from the entire week that you would like to share?

Week Five: Passion for Your Life of Prayer

DAY 25: Warfare Prayer

1. What a journey we have enjoyed as we have explored how to pray and how to grow in our life of prayer. You have spent 30 days focusing on prayer. This is not really an ending, but a beginning as you apply what you've learned on this passionate prayer journey. As you have now finished reading *Passionate Prayer*, what is the most important thing you've learned as a result of the journey? How will this book and its emphasis on walking and talking with God in an intimate relationship with Him make a difference in your life? How has it changed your view of prayer, and how are you motivated to pray?

2. In day 25 you had the opportunity to explore warfare prayer. Why does every believer need to become a prayer warrior?

3. Describe the nature of our spiritual battle. Who and what are our enemies?

4. Describe our spiritual armor and how it protects us.

5. What are your offensive weapons in spiritual warfare?

DAY 26: Intercessory Prayer

1. In day 26 we saw that one of the highest privileges in prayer is interceding on behalf of others. Describe why intercessory prayer is so important.

2. Have you ever prayed for someone else, and if so, what was the result?

3. Has someone ever prayed for you just when you needed it the most? How did those prayers encourage you and help you?

4. How was Moses an example of an intercessor?

5. What was your favorite idea on this day that you would like to try in your own life of prayer?

Day 27: Revival Prayer

1. In day 27, you read about revival prayer. How are you encouraged, knowing that the eyes of the Lord are searching to and fro throughout the earth to strongly support those whose hearts are wholly His?

2. Describe revival prayer and why it is so powerful.

3. How is Ezra an example of revival prayer?

4. What was the most important idea you learned in this day on revival prayer?

Day 28: Effective Prayer

1. In day 28 you saw that the effective prayer of a righteous man can accomplish much. What makes prayer effective?

2. What can effective prayer accomplish? How do you need prayer in your life today?

3. How did the examples encourage you in day 28?

Day 29: The Glory of Prayer

1. In day 29 you took a glimpse into eternity and your future glory. How does knowing you will see the Lord face-to-face encourage you to walk and talk with Him today?

2. How can prayer and the Word of God help you in the darkness of a trial in the same way it helped Charles and Lettie Cowman?

Day 30: The Power of Prayer Quiet Time

1. How does knowing the power of God encourage us to pray?

2. What is the most important truth you learned about God's power? What does His power enable Him to do?

3. As you think about your journey over the last 30 days, what has been most significant to you?

4. What is the most important thing you have learned in this 30-day journey of *Passionate Prayer?* What will you take with you from this time? What is one idea you will incorporate in your life of prayer?

5. Who was your favorite example, or what was your favorite verse or favorite quote?

6. Is there anything else you would like to share as a result of your 30-day journey?

7. Close in prayer.

Appendix 2

MORE RESOURCES FOR PASSIONATE PRAYER

YOUR PRAYER GROWTH PLAN

The following are different aspects of your prayer growth plan.

Adore God in Prayer—see day 7 for example

Prayer Journal—see day 8 for example

Scripture Prayers—see day 8 for example

Listening to God—see day 8 for example

Thank You, Lord—see day 8 for example

Quotes on Prayer—see day 9 for example

Books on Prayer—see day 9 for example

My Adventure in Prayer—see day 10 for example

My Adventure in Knowing God—see day 11 for example

ACTS Example—see day 16 for example

Prayer Focus Example—see day 21 for example

Growing in your life of prayer is a lifelong adventure. Where do you begin? Focus on one aspect at a time as the Lord leads you. These pages are designed to help you organize what God shows you in prayer and what He teaches you in the Word about prayer as He leads you in your prayer growth. Ask yourself periodically, am I praying? Do I talk with God throughout the day? Do I have a regular quiet time, when I can talk with Him about the burdens of my heart? Do I ever open the Bible? Do I have a time, a place, and a plan for my quiet time? What is that plan? Do I ask God before making major decisions?

THIRTY PRAYERS IN THE BIBLE

Many wonderful prayers are included in the Bible. Here are 30 for you to pray when you need them. Memorize each one so they will always be available for you at any time. You might want to meditate on one each day for the next 30 days. You might even look at each verse in other translations, commentaries, and *The Treasury of Scripture Knowledge*. If you have the *Quiet Time Notebook,* you can use a Read and Study page or a Journal page for each verse.

Adoration

"Yours, O Lord, is the greatness and the power and the glory and the victory and the majesty, indeed everything that is in the heavens and the earth; Yours is the dominion, O Lord, and You exalt Yourself as head over all. Both riches and honor come from You, and You rule over all, and in Your hand is power and might; and it lies in Your hand to make great and to strengthen everyone. Now therefore, our God, we thank You, and praise Your glorious name" (1 Chronicles 29:22-24).

"O Lord, our Lord, how majestic is Your name in all the earth, who have displayed Your splendor above the heavens!" (Psalm 8:1).

"I love You, O Lord, my strength" (Psalm 18:1).

"My soul exalts the Lord, and My spirit has rejoiced in God my Savior...For the Mighty One has done great things for me; and holy is His name" (Mary in Luke 1:46-47,49).

"You are my hiding place; You preserve me from trouble; You surround me with songs of deliverance" (Psalm 32:7).

"There is no one holy like the LORD, Indeed, there is no one besides You, nor is there any rock like our God" (1 Samuel 2:2).

"You will make known to me the path of life; in Your presence is fullness of joy; in Your right hand there are pleasures forever" (Psalm 16:11).

"Worthy are You, our Lord and our God, to receive glory and honor and power; for You created all things, and because of Your will they existed, and were created...Worthy is the Lamb that was slain to receive power and riches and wisdom and might and honor and glory and blessing...To Him who sits on the throne, and to the Lamb, be blessing and honor and glory and dominion forever and ever...Amen" (Revelation 4:11; 5:12-14).

Confession

"Create in me a clean heart, O God, and renew a steadfast spirit within me" (Psalm 51:10).

"God, be merciful to me, the sinner!" (Luke 18:13).

"Now behold, I have ventured to speak to the Lord, although I am but dust and ashes" (Abraham in Genesis 18:27).

"O my God, I am ashamed and embarrassed to lift up my face to You, my God, for our iniquities have risen above our heads and our guilt has grown even to the heavens" (Ezra 9:6).

"Search me, O God, and know my heart, try me and know my anxious thoughts; and see if there be any hurtful way in me, and lead me in the everlasting way" (Psalm 139:23-24).

"Plead my cause and redeem me; revive me according to Your word...Great are Your mercies, O LORD; Revive me according to Your ordinances...Consider how I love Your precepts; revive me, O LORD, according to Your lovingkindness" (Psalm 119:154,156,159).

Thanksgiving

"Therefore I will give thanks to You, O LORD, among the nations, and I will sing praises to Your name" (2 Samuel 22:50).

"We give thanks to You, O God, we give thanks, for Your name is near" (Psalm 75:1).

"I will give thanks to You, for I am fearfully and wonderfully made; wonderful are Your works, and my soul knows it very well" (Psalm 139:14).

"Father, I thank you that you heard me. I know that you always hear me" (John 11:41 NCV).

Supplication

"Lord, teach us to pray" (Luke 11:1).

"Give ear to my words, O LORD, consider my groaning. Heed the sound of my cry for help, my King and my God, for to You I pray. In the morning, O LORD, You will hear my voice; in the morning I will order my prayer to You and eagerly watch" (Psalm 5:1-3).

"So teach us to number our days, that we may present to You a heart of wisdom" (Psalm 90:12).

"In You, O LORD, I have taken refuge; let me never be ashamed; in Your righteousness deliver me. Incline Your ear to me, rescue me quickly; be to Me a rock of strength, a stronghold to save me. For You are my rock and my fortress; for Your name's sake You will lead me and guide me" (Psalm 31:1-3).

"Be gracious to me, O LORD, for I am in distress; my eye is wasted away from grief, my soul and my body also…But as for me, I trust in You, O LORD, I say, 'You are my God.' My times are in Your hand; deliver me from the hand of my enemies and from those who persecute me. Make Your face shine upon Your servant; save me in your lovingkindness" (Psalm 31:9,14-16).

"Make me know Your ways, O LORD; teach me Your paths. Lead me in Your truth and teach me, for You are the God of my salvation; for You I wait all the day" (Psalm 25:4-5).

"O LORD, the God of Israel, there is no god like You in heaven or on earth, keeping covenant and showing lovingkindness to Your servants who walk before you with all their heart" (2 Chronicles 6:14).

"Now, O my God, I pray, let Your eyes be open and Your ears attentive to the prayer offered in this place" (2 Chronicles 6:40).

"Sanctify them in the truth; Your word is truth" (John 17:17).

"I know that You can do all things, and that no purpose of Yours can be thwarted...Hear, now, and I will speak; I will ask You, and You instruct me. I have heard of You by hearing of the ear; but now my eye sees You" (Job 42:2,4-5).

"And this I pray, that your love may abound still more and more in real knowledge and all discernment, so that you may approve the things that are excellent, in order to be sincere and blameless until the day of Christ; having been filled with the fruit of righteousness which comes through Jesus Christ, to the glory and praise of God" (Philippians 1:9-11).

"Our Father who is in heaven, hallowed be Your name. Your kingdom come. Your will be done, on earth as it is in heaven. Give us this day our daily bread. And forgive us our debts, as we also have forgiven our debtors. And do not lead us into temptation, but deliver us from evil. For Yours is the kingdom and the power and the glory forever. Amen" (Matthew 6:9-13).

PRAYERS CALLING ON THE NAMES OF GOD

Many wonderful names of God are included in the Bible. The following prayers begin with the names of God and then are open-ended for you to fill in with your own needs as you call on His names. For deeper study in the names of God, see the 30-day journey and the quiet time experience of *Trusting in the Names of God.*

I call on Your name *Elohim,* my God who is triune and created the heavens and the earth...

I call on Your name *El Elyon,* my God who is sovereign and in control of all things…

I call on Your name *Adonai,* my Lord, Master, and Owner…

I call on Your name *El Shaddai,* my God who is all-sufficient…

I call on Your name *Yahweh Jireh,* my Lord who provides everything I need…

I call on Your name *El Ro'i,* my God who sees me…

I call on Your name *Yahweh,* my Lord who is self-existent and everything I need for every circumstance of life…

I call on Your name *Yahweh Rophe,* my Lord who heals me…

I call on Your name *Yahweh Nissi,* my Lord who is my victory…

I call on Your name *Yahweh Mekaddesh,* my Lord who sanctifies me and makes me holy…

I call on Your name *Yahweh Shalom,* my Lord who is my peace and gives me peace…

I call on Your name *Yahweh Sabaoth,* my Lord who is my Deliverer…

I call on Your name *Yahweh Ro'i,* my Lord who is my Shepherd…

I call on Your name *Abba,* Father, my Father in heaven…

MORE PRAYERS IN THE BIBLE FOR FURTHER STUDY

Prayers in the Bible help you learn how the great men and women of God prayed. The following prayers are listed for your further reading and study. This list is certainly not exhaustive but will help you study further. You may want to use the Read and Study page or the Reference Study page in the *Quiet Time Notebook* as a companion for your study. Also, you can study prayer more in-depth with the quiet time experience companion study for *Passionate Prayer.*

Cain's prayer: Genesis 4:13-14

Abraham's prayers: Genesis 15:2; 17:18; 18:23-25; 20:17

Isaac's prayer: Genesis 25:21

Jacob's prayers: Genesis 32:11; 32:24-28

Israelites' prayer: Exodus 2:23

Moses' prayers: Exodus 8:8-9; 15:24-25; 32:31-32; 33:11-23; 34:8-9; Numbers 12:11-13; 27:15-17; Deuteronomy 3:23-25; Psalm 90

Joshua's prayer: Joshua 7:6-9

Manoah's prayer: Judges 13:8

Hannah's prayers: 1 Samuel 1:11; 2:1-10

David's prayers: 1 Samuel 23:10-13; 2 Samuel 7:18; Psalms 3–9; 12–13; 15–18; 21–23; 25–29; 31–41; 51:10-13; 55; 61–65; 68–70; 86; 101; 103; 108–110; 122; 124; 131; 138–145

Solomon's prayers: 2 Chronicles 6:12–7:1; Psalm 72; 127

Sons of Korah prayers: Psalm 42; 44; 46–49; 84–85

Asaph's prayers: Psalms 73–83

Heman the Ezrahite's prayer: Psalm 88

Ethan the Ezrahite's prayer: Psalm 89

More prayers in the psalms: Psalms 91–100; 102; 104; 105–107; 111–121; 125–126; 130; 132; 134–137; 146–150

Elijah's prayer: 1 Kings 17:19-21

Elisha's prayer: 2 Kings 6:17-18

Jehoahaz' prayer: 2 Kings 13:4

Hezekiah's prayers: 2 Kings 19:14-19; 20:3

Jabez' prayer: 1 Chronicles 4:10

Asa's prayer: 2 Chronicles 14:11

Jehoshaphat's prayer: 2 Chronicles 18:31

Manasseh's prayer: 2 Chronicles 33:12-13

Gideon's prayer: Judges 6:36

Ezra's prayer: Ezra 9:6–10:1

Nehemiah's prayer: Nehemiah 1:4-11

Job's prayer: Job 42:1-6

Jeremiah's prayers: Jeremiah 14:7-9; 42:2-6

Daniel's prayer: Daniel 2:17-18; 9:3-5

Jonah's prayer: Jonah 2:1-9

Habakkuk's prayers: Habakkuk 1:2-4; 3:2

Jesus' prayers: Matthew 6:9-13; 11:25; 26:39-44; Luke 23:34,46; John 11:42; 17:1-26

The leper's prayer: Matthew 8:2

The centurion's prayer: Matthew 8:5-6

Peter's prayers: Matthew 14:30; 1 Peter 1:3-5

A woman's prayer: Matthew 15:25

A father's prayer: Mark 9:24

A thief's prayer: Luke 23:42

The disciple's prayer: Acts 4:29-30

Cornelius' prayer: Acts 10:3-4

Paul's prayers: Acts 28:8; Romans 1:8; 1 Corinthians 1:4-8; 2 Corinthians 12:8; Ephesians 1:18-23; 3:14-21; Philippians 1:3-5,9-11; Colossians 1:10-12; 1 Thessalonians 1:2-3; 1 Timothy 1:12

A sinner's prayer: Romans 10:9; 2 Timothy 1:3-4; Philemon 4-6

The author of Hebrews' prayer: Hebrews 13:20-21

Jude's prayer: Jude 24-25

Heaven's prayers: Revelation 4–5

Our prayer: Revelation 22:20

RECOMMENDED READING

Answering God: The Psalms as Tools for Prayer by Eugene Peterson

Becoming a Prayer Warrior: A Guide to Effective and Powerful Prayer by Elizabeth Alves

The Best of Andrew Murray on Prayer by Andrew Murray

Between Heaven and Earth: Prayers and Reflections That Celebrate an Intimate God by Ken Gire

Beyond the Veil by Alice Smith

Breakthrough Prayer: The Secret of Receiving What You Need from God by Jim Cymbala

A Call to Spiritual Reformation: Priorities from Paul and His Prayers by D.A. Carson

Celebration of Discipline: The Path to Spiritual Growth by Richard Foster

A Celebration of Praise: Stand Amazed at Who God Is! by Dick Eastman

Communion with God: Fellowship with Father, Son, and Holy Spirit by John Owen

Daily Communion with God by Matthew Henry

Daily Prayer and Praise: The Book of Psalms Arranged for Private and Family Use by Henry Law

Daily Prayers by F.B. Meyer

Daring to Draw Near: People in Prayer by John White

Dear Abba: Finding the Father's Heart Through Prayer by Claire Cloninger

A Diary of Private Prayer by John Baillie

E.M. Bounds: Man of Prayer by Lyle W. Dorsett

Face to Face: Praying the Scriptures for Intimate Worship by Kenneth Boa

George Mueller of Bristol: His Life of Prayer and Faith by A.T. Pierson

Giving Ourselves to Prayer: An Acts 6:4 Primer for Ministry compiled by Dan R. Crawford

A Guide to Prayer by Isaac Watts

A Guide to Prayer for All God's People by Reuben Job and Norman Shawchuck

The Hidden Life of Prayer by David M'Intyre

How to Pray by R.A. Torrey

If You Will Ask by Oswald Chambers

The Joy of Answered Prayer by D.L. Moody

The Kneeling Christian by an unknown Christian

The Life of Prayer by Edith Schaeffer

Live a Praying Life: Open Your Life to God's Power and Provision by Jennifer Kennedy Dean

Lord, Teach Me to Pray in 28 Days by Kay Arthur

Magnificent Prayer by Nick Harrison

Only a Prayer Meeting by Charles Spurgeon

The Papa Prayer: The Prayer You've Never Prayed by Larry Crabb

The Power of a Praying Wife by Stormie Omartian

The Power of Extraordinary Prayer by Robert Bakke

The Power of Prayer in a Believer's Life by Charles Spurgeon

Prayer by Ole Hallesby

Prayer by James H. McConkey

Prayer: Finding the Heart's True Home by Richard Foster

Prayer on Fire: What Happens When the Holy Spirit Ignites Your Prayers by Fred A. Hartley

Prayer Summits by Joe Aldrich

Prayer, the Great Adventure by David Jeremiah

Prayer Warriors: Powerful Portraits of Soldiers Saints on God's Front Lines by various authors

The Prayers of Peter Marshall by Catherine Marshall

Prayerwalking: Praying On-Site with Insight by Steve Hawthorne and Graham Kendrick

Praying God's Will series by Lee Roberts

Psalms: The Prayer Book of the Bible by Dietrich Bonhoeffer

Quiet Talks on Prayer by S.D. Gordon

Rees Howells: Intercessor by Norman Grubb

Sacred Rhythms: Arranging Our Lives for Spiritual Transformation by Ruth Haley Barton

The Spirit of the Disciplines: Understanding How God Changes Lives by Dallas Willard

Spiritual Disciplines for the Christian Life by Donald S. Whitney

Touching the Heart of God edited by Leonard E. LeSourd

The Transforming Power of Prayer: Deepening Your Friendship with God by James Houston

A Treasury of Prayer: The Best of E.M. Bounds on Prayer in a Single Volume by Leonard Ravenhill, ed.

The Valley of Vision: A Collection of Puritan Prayers and Devotions by Arthur Bennett, ed.

Victorious Praying: Studies in the Family Prayer by Alan Redpath

Waiting on God by Andrew Murray

What Happens When Women Pray by Evelyn Christenson

With Christ in the School of Prayer by Andrew Murray

OTHER RESOURCES FOR YOUR LIFE OF PRAYER

Global Prayer Digest (www.global-prayer-digest.org)

Global Day of Prayer and Seek God for the City (www.way makers.org)

National Day of Prayer (http://www.ndptf.org)

Operation World by Patrick Johnstone and Jason Mandryk (www.operationworld.org)

Prayer shawls (www.tallit.biz, www.theshofarman.com)

The Quiet Time Notebook by Quiet Time Ministries (www.quiet time.org)

"7 Basic Steps to Fasting and Praying" by Dr. Bill Bright (www .billbright.com/7steps/index.html)

Weekly and daily prayer guides by the North American Mission Board (www.namb.net)

NOTES

INTRODUCTION

1. Quoted in Oswald Chambers, *My Utmost for His Highest* (many editions). See the entry for October 17.

2. Quoted in James Houston, *The Transforming Power of Prayer: Deepening Your Friendship with God* (Colorado Springs: NavPress, 1996), 9.

DAY 1

1. Quoted in Larry Crabb, *The Papa Prayer: The Prayer You've Never Prayed* (Nashville: Integrity, 2006), vii.

DAY 2

1. Don Postema, *Space for God: The Study and Practice of Prayer and Spirituality* (Grand Rapids: CRC, 1983), 17.

2. A.W. Tozer, *The Divine Conquest* (New York: Revell, 1950), 22.

3. Eugene Peterson, *The Contemplative Pastor: Returning to the Art of Spiritual Direction* (Carol Stream, IL: Christianity Today International, 1989), 29.

4. Ken Gire, *Between Heaven and Earth: Prayers and Reflections That Celebrate an Intimate God* (San Francisco: HarperSanFrancisco, 1997), v. Used by permission.

DAY 3

1. Quoted in Arthur Bennett, ed., *The Valley of Vision* (Carlisle, PA: The Banner of Truth Trust, 1975), 3. Used by permission.

DAY 4

1. Chambers, *My Utmost for His Highest*. See the entry for October 17.

2. Quoted in S.D. Gordon, *Quiet Talks on Prayer* (New York: Revell, 1904), 141-46.

Day 5

1. Quoted in Eugene Peterson, *Under the Unpredictable Plant: An Exploration in Vocational Holiness* (Grand Rapids: Eerdmans, 1992), 72.

2. Ole Hallesby, *Prayer* (Minneapolis: Augsburg Fortress, 1994), 17.

3. Amy Carmichael, *Mountain Breezes* (Fort Washington: Christian Literature Crusade, 1999), 85. Used by permission.

Day 6

1. Eugene Peterson, *Working the Angles: The Shape of Pastoral Integrity* (Grand Rapids, MI: Eerdmans, 1987), 30-31.

2. Hallesby, *Prayer,* 18.

Day 7

1. R.A. Torrey, *How to Pray* (Chicago: Moody, 2007), 15.

2. To learn about this plan and for more information about how to grow in your quiet time, see my 30-day journey *Six Secrets to a Powerful Quiet Time* (Eugene, OR: Harvest House, 2005).

3. Charles R. Swindoll, *The Tale of the Tardy Oxcart and 1501 Other Stories,* Logos Library System CD ROM (Nashville: Word, 1998).

Day 8

1. Dietrich Bonhoeffer, *Psalms: The Prayer Book of the Bible* (Minneapolis: Augsburg, 1970), 11-12, 15.

2. Lee Roberts, *Praying God's Will for My Husband* (Nashville: Thomas Nelson, 1993).

3. Mother Teresa, *A Simple Path* (New York: Random House, 1995), 7.

4. F.B. Meyer, *Devotional Commentary* (Wheaton: Tyndale House, 1989), 552.

5. Corrie ten Boom with John and Elizabeth Sherrill, *The Hiding Place* (Old Tappan: Revell, 1971), 196-99, 208-9.

Day 10

1. For more on prayer shawls see www.theshofarman.com or www.tallit.biz.

2. Quoted in Postema, *Space for God,* 5.

Day 11

1. Quoted in Claire Cloninger, *Dear Abba: Finding the Father's Heart Through Prayer* (Dallas: Word, 1997), 12-13.

2. To know God more intimately, you may want to read my 30-day journey *Trusting in the Names of God* and the companion book, *Trusting in the Names of God—A Quiet Time Experience* (Eugene, OR: Harvest House, 2008).

DAY 12

1. F.B. Meyer, *Daily Prayers* (Wheaton, IL: Shaw, 1995), 58.

2. Quoted in Mrs. Charles Cowman, *Springs in the Valley* (Los Angeles: The Oriental Missionary Society, 1939), 3-4.

3. Quoted in Cowman, *Springs in the Valley,* 3-4.

DAY 13

1. Hallesby, *Prayer,* 18-26.

2. Quoted in Cowman, *Streams in the Desert* (Los Angeles: Oriental Mission Society, 1925), 374-75.

3. Charles Spurgeon, "Man's Extremity, God's Opportunity," in *Spurgeon's Sermons,* vol. 47, sermon 2717.

4. Charles Spurgeon, "A New Song for New Hearts," in *Spurgeon's Sermons,* vol. 16, sermon 928.

DAY 14

1. Matthew Henry and Thomas Scott, *Matthew Henry's Concise Commentary* (Oak Harbor, WA: Logos Research Systems CD ROM, 1997). See the entry for Psalm 119:66.

2. Chambers, *My Utmost for His Highest.* See the entry for May 3.

DAY 15

1. Quoted in David McCasland, *Oswald Chambers: Abandoned to God* (Nashville: Discovery House, 1993), 120.

2. Norman Grubb, *Rees Howells: Intercessor* (Fort Washington: Christian Literature Crusade, 1952), 114.

3. E.M. Bounds, *Power Through Prayer* (Minneapolis: World Wide Publications, 1989), 57.

DAY 16

1. Andrew Murray, *With Christ in the School of Prayer* (Old Tappan, NJ: Revell, 1979), 14.

2. For example, Larry Chouinard, *Matthew,* in *The College Press NIV Commentary* (Joplin, MO: College Press, 1997), (see the entry for Matthew 6:9); James Montgomery Boice, *The Gospel of Matthew* (Grand Rapids: Baker Books, 2001), 99.

3. Kenneth L. Barker, ed., *The TNIV Study Bible* (Grand Rapids: Zondervan, 2006), 1619.

4. Paul Ellingworth and Eugene A. Nida, *A Handbook on the Letter to the Hebrews,* UBS Handbook: Helps for Translators (New York: United Bible Societies, 1994), 98.

5. E.M. Bounds, *The Reality of Prayer* (Grand Rapids: Baker, 1991), 32.

DAY 17

1. D.A. Carson, *A Call to Spiritual Reformation: Priorities from Paul and His Prayers* (Grand Rapids: Baker, 1992), 224.

2. Carson, *A Call to Spiritual Reformation,* 224.

DAY 18

1. John Oxenham, *Bees in Amber.* Available online at www.gutenberg.org.
2. Gordon, *Quiet Talks on Prayer,* 214-16.
3. Quoted in Carson, *A Call to Spiritual Reformation,* 16.
4. Quoted in Cowman, *Streams in the Desert,* 327.

DAY 19

1. For more encouragement on embracing God's promises, see my book *Walking with the God Who Cares* (Eugene, OR: Harvest House, 2007).
2. Cowman, *Streams in the Desert,* 356-57.
3. Gire, *Between Heaven and Earth,* 98-100.

DAY 20

1. Pierson, *George Mueller of Bristol,* 140-41.

DAY 21

1. James Montgomery Boice, *The Sermon on the Mount* (Grand Rapids: Baker, 2002), 235.
2. A.W. Tozer, *The Knowledge of the Holy* (New York: Harper & Row, 1961), 89.
3. Hannah Whitall Smith, *The God of All Comfort* (Chicago: Moody Press, 1956), 95.
4. George Mueller, *Autobiography of George Mueller,* comp. by G. Fred Bergin (London: Nisbet, 1906), 424. Quoted in John Piper, *The Pleasures of God* (Portland: Multnomah Press, 1991), 189-90.
5. Pierson, *George Mueller of Bristol,* 238.

DAY 22

1. Chambers, *My Utmost for His Highest.* See the entry for May 3.
2. Crabb, *The Papa Prayer,* 46.
3. C.E.B. Cranfield, *Romans: A Shorter Commentary* (Grand Rapids: Eerdmans, 1985), 202.
4. William R. Newell, *Romans Verse by Verse: A Classic Evangelical Commentary* (Chicago: Moody Press, 1977), 326.
5. Quoted in Leonard E. LeSourd, ed., *Touching the Heart of God* (Grand Rapids: Chosen Books, 1990), 26.
6. LeSourd, *Touching the Heart of God,* 28-29.

DAY 23

1. Renée Bondi, *The Last Dance but Not the Last Song* (Grand Rapids: Revell, 2002), 224.
2. Bondi, *The Last Dance but Not the Last Song,* 225.
3. Gordon D. Fee: *Philippians,* The IVP New Testament Commentary Series (Downers Grove, IL: InterVarsity Press, 1999), 174.
4. Quoted in Peter Thomas O'Brian, *The Epistle to the Philippians: A Commentary on the Greek Text* (Grand Rapids: Eerdmans, 1991), 492.

5. "Be Not Afraid" © 1975, 1978 by Robert J. Dufford, SJ and OCP Publications, 5536 NE Hassalo, Portland, OR 97213. All rights reserved. Used by permission.

DAY 24

1. Gire, *Between Heaven and Earth,* 155-56.

DAY 25

1. J. Vernon McGee, *Ephesians,* vol. 47 of *Thru the Bible Commentary* (Nashville: Thomas Nelson, 1991), 186.

2. For an in-depth study of the Holy Spirit, see my book *Set My Heart on Fire: Experience the Power of the Holy Spirit* (Eugene: Harvest House, 2008).

3. Chambers, *My Utmost for His Highest.* See the entry for October 30.

4. Chambers, *My Utmost for His Highest,.* See the entry for October 17.

5. Charles Spurgeon, *Morning and Evening* (Peabody, MAA: Hendrickson, 2006). See the morning entry for June 2.

DAY 26

1. Elizabeth Alves, *Becoming a Prayer Warrior* (Ventura, CA: Renew, 1998), 29-30.

2. Quoted in Leonard Ravenhill, *Revival God's Way* (Minneapolis: Bethany House, 1983), 112.

DAY 27

1. Taken from J. Edwin Orr's message "The Role of Prayer In Spiritual Awakening," delivered at the National Prayer Congress in Dallas, Texas, October 26-29, 1976.

2. Quoted in Cowman, *Streams in the Desert,* 359-60.

DAY 28

1. Henry and Scott, *Matthew Henry's Concise Commentary.*

DAY 29

1. Cowman, *Springs in the Valley,* 367-69.

2. Cowman, *Springs in the Valley,* 368.

3. Annie Johnson Flint, *Best Loved Poems* (Toronto: Evangelical Publishers, n.d.), 42.

DAY 30

1. Gire, *Between Heaven and Earth,* 354.

2. Quoted in Gire, *Between Heaven and Earth,* 354.

3. Quoted in Gire, *Between Heaven and Earth,* 101.

4. Quoted in Gire, *Between Heaven and Earth,* 353.

About the Author

Catherine Martin is a summa cum laude graduate of Bethel Theological Seminary with a master of arts degree in theological studies. She is founder of Quiet Time Ministries, a director of women's ministries, and a member of the adjunct faculty of Biola University. Teaching at retreats and conferences, she challenges others to seek God and love Him with all of their heart, soul, mind, and strength.

About Quiet Time Ministries

Quiet Time Ministries teaches devotion to God and Word to men and women throughout the world. Contact us for more information.

Quiet Time Ministries
PO Box 14007
Palm Desert, CA 92255
1-800-925-6458
www.quiettime.org